Kivy Cookbook

Enhance your skills in developing multitouch applications with Kivy

Hugo Solis

BIRMINGHAM - MUMBAI

Kivy Cookbook

First published: August 2015

Production reference: 1170815

Published by Packt Publishing Ltd.
Livery Place
35 Livery Street
Birmingham B3 2PB, UK.

ISBN 978-1-78398-738-2

www.packtpub.com

Credits

Author

Hugo Solis

Reviewers

Davide Depau

Abhinav Jangda

Matt Lebrun

Patrick Louis

Commissioning Editor

Usha Iyer

Acquisition Editor

Richard Gall

Content Development Editor

Mamata Walkar

Technical Editor

Tejaswita Karvir

Copy Editor

Dipti Mankame

Project Coordinator

Shipra Chawhan

Proofreader

Safis Editing

Indexer

Priya Sane

Graphics

Sheetal Aute

Production Coordinator

Shantanu N. Zagade

Cover Work

Shantanu N. Zagade

About the Author

Hugo Solis is an assistant professor in the physics department at the University of Costa Rica. In the same institution, he collaborates with CITIC and CICIMA. His current research interests include computational cosmology, complexity, and the influence of hydrogen on material properties. He has wide experience in languages, including C/C++ and Python for scientific programming and visualization. He is a member of the Free Software Foundation and has contributed code to some free software projects. He has also been a technical reviewer for *Mastering Object-oriented Python*, *Kivy: Interactive Applications in Python*, and *Learning Object-Oriented Programming* by Packt Publishing. Currently, he is in charge of the IFT, a Costa Rican scientific nonprofit organization for the multidisciplinary practice of physics (http://iftucr.org).

I would like to thank God for this life and all his blessings. One of those blessings is my beloved mother, Katty Sanchez, whom I have to thank for her support and vanguard thoughts.

I am grateful to my amazing friends Laura Rojas, Jose David Cojal, Gerardo Lacy, Allan Lacy, Pamela Saborio, and Ana Segura for sharing this long ride in the life with me.

A special thanks to my professors, colleagues, and friends—Manuel Ortega, Daniel Azofeifa, Neville Clark, William Vargas, Max Chaves, and Gabriela Barrantes—and MICITT and CONICIT for supporting my PhD studies.

I would also like to thank my brothers, Harry and Geancarlo, for enduring a geek brother, and Helena Oses for her endearment and unique words.

I owe the most to all the people behind Kivy, Python, and Packt Publishing. Thank you.

About the Reviewers

Abhinav Jangda has a deep interest in the field of application development. He is an open source enthusiast. He has contributed to open source projects, including Kivy and GNOME. He was one of the main contributors to the development of Kivy designer. He has been using Kivy as his primary application development framework. Besides Python, he has developed applications in C, C++, Java, and C# using some framework, such as GTK+, Qt, Java SWT, and Windows Presentation Foundation. He has been researching in the fields of operating systems, compilers, and virtual machines. He loves working with Linux and developing applications for it.

Matt Lebrun is a software engineer from the Philippines. He recalls his first dibs in programming using QBasic when he was 13, and since then, he's only gone deeper into this sleep-depriving yet overly rewarding field.

After college education, he started his career customizing in-house and commercial ERP systems. Then, he moved on to telecoms support systems, where he mainly dabbled with C++, Perl, and Shell scripts.

Nowadays, he's making up for lost times with his passion for hacking on data-oriented and web-related technologies through Python and Django in Save22 Inc.

On his days off, you'll catch him volunteering for the local Python community, hacking on a side project with his girlfriend, or in hermit mode learning something new.

> I would like to thank my girlfriend, Mickey, for supporting me in writing this book review.

Patrick Louis is an advocate of the *learn by/from curiosity* movement. For him, programming is just another way of expression—an art. He likes to contribute his free time to the open source projects that catch his attention. He's a core member of the nixers.net community.

www.PacktPub.com

Support files, eBooks, discount offers, and more

For support files and downloads related to your book, please visit www.PacktPub.com.

Did you know that Packt offers eBook versions of every book published, with PDF and ePub files available? You can upgrade to the eBook version at www.PacktPub.com and as a print book customer, you are entitled to a discount on the eBook copy. Get in touch with us at service@packtpub.com for more details.

At www.PacktPub.com, you can also read a collection of free technical articles, sign up for a range of free newsletters and receive exclusive discounts and offers on Packt books and eBooks.

https://www2.packtpub.com/books/subscription/packtlib

Do you need instant solutions to your IT questions? PacktLib is Packt's online digital book library. Here, you can search, access, and read Packt's entire library of books.

Why Subscribe?

- ▸ Fully searchable across every book published by Packt
- ▸ Copy and paste, print, and bookmark content
- ▸ On demand and accessible via a web browser

Free Access for Packt account holders

If you have an account with Packt at www.PacktPub.com, you can use this to access PacktLib today and view 9 entirely free books. Simply use your login credentials for immediate access.

Table of Contents

Preface

The book is full of practical task-based recipes to be performed while developing multitouch applications with Kivy. The focus of this book is to guide you through the Kivy framework to develop apps and get your apps ready for distribution in App Stores and Android devices. We'll focus on common, real-world scenarios. You'll be able to leverage these recipes right away, which allows you to create most diverse apps and learn how to distribute them using the Kivy framework, and widen your proficiency in developing multitouch applications with Kivy.

What this book covers

Chapter 1, *Kivy and the Kv Language*, introduces the Python code, Kv language, widgets, and Kivy garden. The topics covered in this chapter lay the foundation for the remaining code samples in each chapter.

Chapter 2, *Input, Motion, and Touch*, demonstrates some of the most common recipient-related management tasks, such as evolving to the touchscreen, using the gyroscope, and detecting multitapping. You'll also learn how to recognize touch shapes, record gestures, and differentiate between touch and motion events.

Chapter 3, *Events*, shows how to schedule a one-time event and a repetitive event. Triggering events, defining widget events, creating custom events are also covered in this chapter.

Chapter 4, *Widgets*, covers the manipulation of widget tree, traversing of tree. It also covers the FloatLayout, BoxLayout, StackLayout, AnchorLayout, and action bar.

Chapter 5, *Graphics – Canvas and Instructions*, explains various methods, such as separating with the screen manager, using context instructions, and using drawing instructions. You'll learn how to modify with multitouching and storing and retrieving the coordinate space context.

Chapter 6, *Advancing Graphics – Shaders and Rendering*, covers Carousel, layouts, and shaders. The other topics covered in this chapter are rendering in a Framebuffer and optimizing graphics.

Chapter 7, *The API in Detail*, introduces API and covers the logging objects, parsing, applying utils, using spelling, adding effects, and adding text.

Chapter 8, *Packaging our Apps for PC*, shows how to perform packing for Windows, Linux, and MacOs. It also shows multimedia for Windows and running apps in Windows and MacOS.

Chapter 9, *Kivy for Mobile Devices*, explains various methods, such as packaging for iOS and resizing the screen into iOS. You'll learn preparing for the App Store, packaging for Android, and resizing the screen into Android.

What you need for this book

To complete the recipes in this book, you'll need the following:

- Kivy 1.9.0
- Cross-platform
- Windows/OS X/Linux
- iOS device / Android device
- iOS and OS X / Android and Linux

Who this book is for

This book is intended for developers who want to use features of the Kivy framework and develop multitouch applications. Prior experience with Kivy is not required although familiarity with Python is expected.

Sections

In this book, you will find several headings that appear frequently (Getting ready, How to do it, How it works, There's more, and See also).

To give clear instructions on how to complete a recipe, we use these sections as follows:

Getting ready

This section tells you what to expect in the recipe, and describes how to set up any software or any preliminary settings required for the recipe.

How to do it...

This section contains the steps required to follow the recipe.

How it works...

This section usually consists of a detailed explanation of what happened in the previous section.

There's more...

This section consists of additional information about the recipe in order to make the reader more knowledgeable about the recipe.

See also

This section provides helpful links to other useful information for the recipe.

Conventions

In this book, you will find a number of text styles that distinguish between different kinds of information. Here are some examples of these styles and an explanation of their meaning.

Code words in text, database table names, folder names, filenames, file extensions, pathnames, dummy URLs, user input, and Twitter handles are shown as follows: "We are using again our KV file with a simple button and empty label with ID `button1` and `label1` respectively"

A block of code is set as follows:

```
<MyW>:
    Button:
        id: button1
        text: 'Hello'
        on_press: root.animate(button1)
```

When we wish to draw your attention to a particular part of a code block, the relevant lines or items are set in bold:

```
canvas.after:
    PopMatrix
```

Any command-line input or output is written as follows:

```
$ Kivy pyinstaller.py --windowed --name e1
/Users/Me/Documents/e1app/e1.py
```

New terms and **important words** are shown in bold. Words that you see on the screen, for example, in menus or dialog boxes, appear in the text like this: "We are going to use one simple Python files that will just show our **Hello World** text"

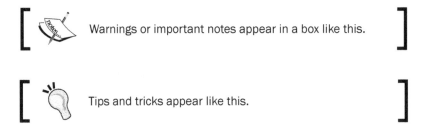

Warnings or important notes appear in a box like this.

Tips and tricks appear like this.

Reader feedback

Feedback from our readers is always welcome. Let us know what you think about this book—what you liked or disliked. Reader feedback is important for us as it helps us develop titles that you will really get the most out of.

To send us general feedback, simply e-mail feedback@packtpub.com, and mention the book's title in the subject of your message.

If there is a topic that you have expertise in and you are interested in either writing or contributing to a book, see our author guide at www.packtpub.com/authors.

Customer support

Now that you are the proud owner of a Packt book, we have a number of things to help you to get the most from your purchase.

Downloading the example code

You can download the example code files from your account at http://www.packtpub.com for all the Packt Publishing books you have purchased. If you purchased this book elsewhere, you can visit http://www.packtpub.com/support and register to have the files e-mailed directly to you.

Errata

Although we have taken every care to ensure the accuracy of our content, mistakes do happen. If you find a mistake in one of our books—maybe a mistake in the text or the code—we would be grateful if you could report this to us. By doing so, you can save other readers from frustration and help us improve subsequent versions of this book. If you find any errata, please report them by visiting http://www.packtpub.com/submit-errata, selecting your book, clicking on the **Errata Submission Form** link, and entering the details of your errata. Once your errata are verified, your submission will be accepted and the errata will be uploaded to our website or added to any list of existing errata under the Errata section of that title.

To view the previously submitted errata, go to https://www.packtpub.com/books/content/support and enter the name of the book in the search field. The required information will appear under the **Errata** section.

Piracy

Piracy of copyrighted material on the Internet is an ongoing problem across all media. At Packt, we take the protection of our copyright and licenses very seriously. If you come across any illegal copies of our works in any form on the Internet, please provide us with the location address or website name immediately so that we can pursue a remedy.

Please contact us at copyright@packtpub.com with a link to the suspected pirated material.

We appreciate your help in protecting our authors and our ability to bring you valuable content.

Questions

If you have a problem with any aspect of this book, you can contact us at questions@packtpub.com, and we will do our best to address the problem.

1
Kivy and the Kv Language

In this first chapter, we will cover the following recipes:

- ▶ Installing Kivy
- ▶ Building your interfaces
- ▶ Declaring properties within a class
- ▶ Relating the Python code and the Kv language
- ▶ Referencing widgets
- ▶ Accessing widgets defined inside the Kv language in your Python code
- ▶ Reusing styles in multiple widgets
- ▶ Designing with the Kv language
- ▶ Running your code
- ▶ Using Kivy garden

Introduction

The first chapter is going to introduce the reader to the **Kivy framework**, its basis, and the **Kv language**. This is necessary work and a common base for the next chapters. If this is your first time using Kivy, it is advised that you do not skip this chapter. However, if you do, remember to return to this chapter if you need to install a supporting tool or verify any concept that you need to support your current solution.

Installing Kivy

This recipe will teach you how to install Kivy on a personal computer, which is the first step in starting to develop great software.

Getting ready

We will assume that you already have GNU/Linux (preferably Ubuntu/Debian/Trisquel, we recommend the last one) and Python installed on it. Usually, Python is already installed on the aforementioned GNU/Linux distributions. We will also assume that you are using Python version 2.7 or higher.

How to do it...

1. Add one of the **Personal Package Archives** (**PPAs**) that you prefer; our recommendation is the following stable one:

   ```
   stable builds:  $ sudo add-apt-repository ppa:kivy-
   team/kivy
   ```

   ```
   nightly builds: $ sudo add-apt-repository ppa:kivy-
   team/kivy-daily
   ```

2. Update your package list using your package manager:

   ```
   $ sudo apt-get update
   ```

3. Install Python-kivy and, optionally, the examples that are found in Python-kivy-examples:

   ```
   $ sudo apt-get install Python-kivy
   ```

4. Verify the installation. Call Python from the console and execute this command:

   ```
   import kivy
   ```

How it works...

There are many ways to get Kivy installed on your computer. Here we are describing probably the easiest way using your distribution's package manager. In the first step, we are adding a PPA as an **APT repository** to provide you with two different options: the stable one, for which all the Kivy products have been well tested, and the nightly one, which are packages under active development. Actually, for Ubuntu, you can skip the first step; it was just to get the latest version of Kivy.

In the second step, we update the list of available packages to include the Kivy repository. The third step is where the installation of Kivy really happens by using the distribution's package manager. In the last step, we verify if Kivy is working with the command that imports Kivy. If everything is OK we will see the following:

```
[INFO  ] Kivy v1.9.0
```

It shows the Kivy version that you installed in your system, which is v1.9.0 in this case. Remember to exit Python, for which we use the command quit().

There's more...

Now we will say something about Mac OS X and Microsoft Windows; for them, Kivy provides what is called portable packages. For an easy way to get Kivy running, just go to http://kivy.org/#download.

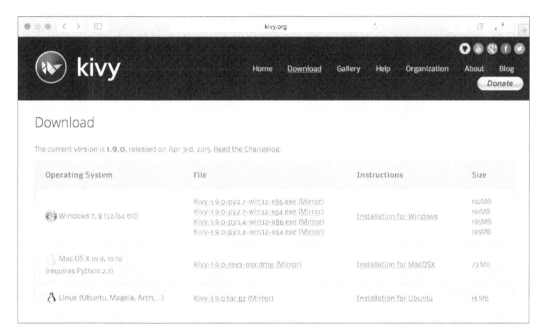

Mac OS X

Download the `dmg` file, double-click to open it, and drag the Kivy.app into your Applications folder. Ready!

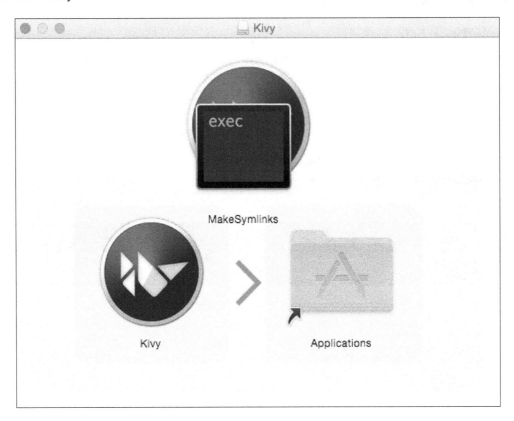

You should run the **make-symlinks** script to make Kivy available in the shell system. Thus, you can run Kivy from the terminal.

Microsoft Windows

Download the `.zip` file and unzip it. There is a file named `kivy.bat` that must be copied as a shortcut into your `SendTo` folder.

See also

Well, if you are using a different operating system, you are always able to go to `http://kivy.org/#download` and look for the one that you are using. Also, if you want to build Kivy from the source code, refer to *Chapter 8, Packaging our Apps for PC* the recipe *Packing for Linux*.

Building your interfaces

Now we are going to create an interface, a very simple one, providing some basics in the developing of Kivy interfaces.

Getting ready

We are going to start to develop our first application with Kivy, and we need an editor for coding; you can use your favorite for Python without any problem. Here, we are using gedit, just because it comes with almost all GNU/Linux distros.

How to do it...

These steps will generate our first Kivy interface:

1. Open a new file in gedit and save it as `e1.py`.
2. Import the Kivy framework.
3. Subclass the `App` class.
4. Implement its `build()` method, so it returns a widget instance (the root of your widget tree).
5. Instantiate this class and call its `run()` method.

The code for this is as follows:

```
import kivy
kivy.require('1.9.0') # Kivy ver where the code has been tested!

from kivy.app import App
from kivy.uix.label import Label

class MyApp(App):
    def build(self):
        return Label(text='Hello world')

if __name__ == '__main__':
    MyApp().run()
```

How it works...

Well, let's see the code in detail; the first line is:

```
import kivy
```

This does the magic of linking Python with Kivy. The second line is optional:

```
kivy.require('1.9.0')
```

However, it is extremely useful because it prevents version conflicts; if you have an old Kivy version, you will have to update to at least the version that is required. In the third line:

```
from kivy.app import App
```

It is required that the base class of your app inherits from the `App` class, which is present in the `kivy_installation_dir/kivy/app.py` folder. This is to connect your app with the Kivy GUI. The fourth line is:

```
from kivy.uix.label import Label
```

The `uix` module is the section that holds the user interface elements, such as layouts and widgets. This is a very common import that you will use in the future. Moving on to the fifth line:

```
class MyApp(App):
```

This is where we define the base class of our Kivy app. You should only ever need to change the name of your app `MyApp` in this line. The sixth line is:

```
def build(self):
```

This is the function where you should initialize and return your root widget. This is what we do on the seventh line:

```
return Label(text='Hello world')
```

Here we initialize a `Label` with the text `Hello World` and return its instance. This label is the root widget of this app.

Now, on to the portion that makes our app come to life is in the eighth and ninth lines:

```
if __name__ == '__main__':
MyApp().run()
```

Here, the class `MyApp` is initialized, and its `run()` method is called. This initializes and starts our Kivy app.

There's more...

Something to point out is the name of the window, it will be called `My` because of the name of the base class. Ergo, if you want the title of the window be `Win1`, your base class must be `Win1App`. So, the fifth line would be:

```
class Win1App(App):
```

You must change the last one to:

```
Win1App().run()
```

Actually, a suffix of `App` isn't necessary; it is just commonly used in Kivy. If you want to include an `App` suffix in the title or spaces, override the title attribute as:

```
class Win1App(App):
    def build(self):
        self.title = 'Win 1 App'
```

See also

If you want to run your interface, take a look at our recipe *Running your code*. Also you can take a look in the file `kivy_installation_dir/kivy/app.py`, which is a very good document to go deeper into Kivy apps.

Declaring properties within a class

Here we want to highlight an important difference between traditional Python coding and Kivy, and the usefulness of this change.

Getting ready

We need to remember the traditional form to declare properties in Python. Usually, if we want to declare a property in Python, we do something such as:

```
class MyClass(object):
    def __init__(self):
        super(MyClass,self).__init__()
        self._numeric_var = 1
    @property
    def numeric_var(self):
        return self._numeric_var
```

We are declaring a numeric one, whereas if we use `MyClass().numeric_var` in the Python shell, we get `1` in return.

How to do it...

Now, to declare this property in Kivy we follow these steps:

1. Import Kivy and its properties
2. Define the class
3. Reference the Kivy property, in this case the numeric one:

```
import kivy

from kivy.event import EventDispatcher
from kivy.properties import *

class MyClass(EventDispatcher):
    numeric_var = NumericProperty(1.0)
```

How it works...

The idea behind this is that you inherit the declaration from Kivy's properties, which reduces the number of code lines.

To use them, you have to declare them at a class level. That is, directly in the class, not in any method for the class. A property is a class attribute that will automatically create instance attributes. Each property, by default, provides an `on_<propertyname>` event that is called whenever the property's state/value changes.

Something additional to point out is that **NumericProperty** accepts all the Python numeric values: ints, floats, and longs.

In general, Kivy properties can be overridden easily when creating the instance of the class, using keyword arguments such as `ClassName(property=newvalue)`.

There's more...

They help you to:

▶ Easily manipulate widgets defined in the Kv language
▶ Automatically observe any changes
▶ Check and validate values
▶ Optimize memory management

Kivy provides more properties as follows:

- NumericProperty
- StringProperty
- ListProperty
- ObjectProperty
- BooleanProperty
- BoundedNumericProperty
- OptionProperty
- ReferenceListProperty
- AliasProperty
- DictProperty

See also

These properties actually implement the Observer pattern; if you want to learn more about patterns, you can find information online at `http://www.oodesign.com/observer-pattern.html`.

Relating Python code and the Kv language

This recipe will teach you how to relate the Kv language to Python code. Kivy provides a design language specifically geared toward easy and scalable GUI design. The Kv language separates the interface design from the application logic, adhering to the separation of concerns principle, where the application remains in Python and the design remains in the Kv language.

Getting ready

This recipe will create the same interface as the recipe *Building your interfaces*, but now using the Kv language; hence, it could be educational to look the code in there to make some comparisons. Again we are using gedit, just because it comes with almost all GNU/Linux distros.

How to do it...

These steps will generate our Kivy interface using the Kv language:

1. Open a new file in gedit and save it as `e4.py`.
2. Make a rule for the label.
3. Provide the text for the label:

   ```
   <Label>:
       text: 'Hello World'
   ```

4. Open a new file in gedit and save it as `e4.py`.
5. Import the Kivy framework.
6. Provide a subclass to the `App` class.
7. Implement its `build()` method, so it returns a widget instance.
8. Instantiate this class and call its `run()` method:

   ```
   import kivy
   kivy.require('1.9.0') # Kivy ver where the code has been
   tested!
   from kivy.app import App
   from kivy.uix.label import Label
   class e4App(App):
       def build(self):
           return Label()

   if __name__ == '__main__':
       e4App().run()
   ```

How it works...

Well, let's see the code in detail. The first line for the file `e4.kv` is:

   `<Label>:`

This line creates the rule for a `Label`. The second one is:

   `text: 'Hello World'`

In this, we define the text property for the `Label` with the value `'Hello World'`.

Now, the first four lines of the Python file are the common ones to use Kivy in Python, and we already reviewed them in this chapter recipe *Building your Interfaces*. Moving on to the fifth line:

   `class e4App(App):`

This is where we define the base class of our Kivy app. You should only ever need to change the name of your app `e4App` in this line, and here is where the relationship between the Kv language and the Python code occurs. What happens is that Kivy looks for a file named `e4.kv`, which could be present or not. The sixth line is:

```
def build(self):
```

This is the function where you initialize and return your root widget. This is what we do on the seventh line:

```
return Label()
```

Here we initialize a `Label` and returned its instance. This `Label` is the root widget of this app, and it must be the same in the KV file.

Now, on to the portion that makes our app come to life is in the eighth and ninth lines:

```
if __name__ == '__main__':
    e4App().run()
```

Here, the class `e4App` is initialized, and its `run()` method is called. This initializes and starts our Kivy app.

There's more...

The filename of the KV file should be such that adding the name of the KV file and `App` will become the name of the subclass of the `App` class. For example, if you change the name to `Win1App`, then you should also change the KV filename to `Win1.kv`.

Something to point out is that we can incorporate the KV code inside the Python file with the class `Builder`. We just add a few lines between the fourth and fifth lines in the Python code to import the Builder package and the override of the method as follows:

```
from kivy.lang import Builder
Builder.load_string('''
    <Label>:
        text: 'Hello World'
''')
```

See also

If you want to run your interface, take a look at our recipe *Running your Code* and compare the result with the recipe *Building your Interfaces*.

Referencing widgets

Sometimes, it is necessary to access or reference other widgets in a specific widget tree. In the Kv language, there is a way to do it using IDs.

Getting ready

This recipe will use two common widgets just for reference. The `Button` and `TextInput` fields are very common widgets.

How to do it...

This recipe is as follows:

1. Make a rule
2. Establish the ID
3. Call the ID:

```
<MyWidget>:
    Button:
        id: f_but
    TextInput:
        text: f_but.state
```

How it works...

Let's see the code; this is the first line:

```
<MyWidget>:
```

This is the name of the widget we will use, which is a clickable text input. The second line is:

```
Button:
```

This defines the button. The third line is:

```
id: f_but
```

This gives the button an ID of `f_but`, which we will use to reference the button. The fourth line is:

```
TextInput:
```

This defines the text input. The fifth line is:

```
text: f_but.state
```

This is the definition of the text that is in the text input where we are referencing the state of the button. It says that if you do not click the button, the text in the text input is normal, and if you click the button, the text in the text input is shown.

There's more...

An ID is limited in scope to the rule it is declared in, so in the preceding code, f_but cannot be accessed outside the <MyWidget> rule; that is, if we have a second <MyWidget2>, we are not able to reference f_but in <MyWidget2>.

Also ID is a weakref module for the widget and not the widget itself. As a consequence, storing the ID is not sufficient to keep the widget from being garbage collected. To demonstrate:

```
<MyWidget>:
    label_widget: label_widget.__self__
    Button:
        text: 'Add Button'
        on_press: root.add_widget(label_widget)
    Button:
        text: 'Remove Button'
        on_press: root.remove_widget(label_widget)
    Label:
        id: label_widget
        text: 'widget'
```

If we do not use ID.__self__ or in this case label_widget.__self__ just label_widget, we are going to get an error: **ReferenceError: weakly-referenced object no longer exists**.

See also

If you want to get more details about widgets, see the recipes in *Chapter 4, Widgets*.

Accessing widgets defined inside the Kv language in your Python code

This recipe will teach you how to access definitions inside the Kv language in your Python code and vice versa.

Getting ready

This recipe will use button, a very common widget that we also used in the last recipe.

How to do it...

This recipe follows as:

1. Make a rule for the widget.
2. Define a button.
3. Give it an ID.
4. Define the label for the button.
5. In the action, call a method in the Python code:

```
<MyW>:
    Button:
        id: b1
        text: 'Press to smash'
        on_release: root.b_smash()
```

6. Create the Python code with the method:

```
import kivy
kivy.require('1.8.0') # replace with your current kivy version !

from kivy.app import App
from kivy.uix.widget import Widget

class MyW(Widget):
    def b_smash(self):
        self.ids.b1.text = 'Pudding'

class e7App(App):
    def build(self):
        return MyW()

if __name__ == '__main__':
    e7App().run()
```

How it works...

In the Kv Language file, we have the following in the first line:

```
<MyW>:
```

This is the name of the widget, a simple button. The second line is:

```
Button:
```

This is the button definition. The third line is:

```
id: b1
```

This gives the button an ID b1. The fourth line is:

```
text: 'Press to smash'
```

This makes the initial text on the button 'Press to smash'. The fifth line is:

```
on_release: root.b_smash()
```

The preceding line is making a call to the Python code; it refers the method b_smash() of the root class MyW.

The fifth line in the Python code is:

```
class MyW(Widget):
```

This is the definition of the class related to the Widget. The sixth line is:

```
def b_smash(self):
```

This defines the method b_smash(), which is accessed by the Kv language file.
The seventh line is:

```
self.ids.b1.text = 'Pudding'
```

This accesses the widget defined in the Kv language file, specifically the button with its ID, and changes the text displayed in the button to the text Pudding.

See also

If you want to run your interface, take a look at our recipe *Running your code*, and to get more details about widgets, see the recipes in *Chapter 4, Widgets*.

Reusing styles in multiple widgets

This recipe will teach you how to take advantage of reusing styles for different widgets, a procedure that could be useful for the scalability of a system.

Getting ready

We will use this example of a file, `e8.kv`, where two widgets are defined:

```
<MyWidget1>:
    Button:
        on_press: self.text(txt_inpt.text)
    TextInput:
        id: txt_inpt
<MyWidget2>:
    Button:
        on_press: self.text(txt_inpt.text)
    TextInput:
        id: txt_inpt
```

We must note that they are very similar, and actually just the name of the widget is different between them.

How to do it...

The following steps provide a way to join the two widgets:

-   Let's conserve just one of the widgets.
-   The name of the discarded widget will be added to name of the conserved widget, by separating with a comma:

```
<MyWidget1,MyWidget2>:
    Button:
        on_press: self.text(txt_inpt.text)
    TextInput:
        id: txt_inpt
```

How it works...

In this case, by separating the class names with a comma, all the classes listed in the declaration will have the same KV properties and you could join any number of similar widgets.

There's more...

In the Python code, the widgets could do different tasks, as in the next portion of code:

```
class MyWidget1(Widget):
    def text(self, val):
        print('text input text is: {txt}'.format(txt=val))
class MyWidget2(Widget):
    writing = StringProperty('')
    def text(self, val): self.writing = val
```

Similarly, you can join the widgets in the Kv language.

See also

If you want to get more details about widgets, see the recipes in *Chapter 4, Widgets*.

Designing with the Kv language

This recipe will give you a first look at the widgets' distribution and their interaction.

Getting ready

This recipe will use two common widgets, just for reference; again we'll be looking at the Button and TextInput fields. Also, a common kind of layout is BoxLayout, which controls the distribution of objects in the interface.

How to do it...

This recipe works by performing the following steps:

1. First, the KV file:

    ```
    <Controller>:
        label_wid: my_custom_label

        BoxLayout:
            orientation: 'horizontal'
            padding: 20

            Button:
                text: 'My controller info is: ' + root.info
                on_press: root.do_action()
    ```

```
        Label:
            id: my_custom_label
            text: 'My label before button press'
```

2. Next, the Python code:

```python
import kivy
kivy.require('1.8.0')

from kivy.uix.floatlayout import FloatLayout
from kivy.app import App
from kivy.properties import ObjectProperty, StringProperty

class Controller(FloatLayout):

    label_wid = ObjectProperty()
    info = StringProperty()

    def do_action(self):
        self.label_wid.text = 'Button pressed'
        self.info = 'Bye'

class e8App(App):
    def build(self):
        return Controller(info='Hello world')
if __name__ == '__main__':
    e0App().run()
```

How it works...

If we are designing with the Kv language, let's see it in detail. In the first line:

<Controller>:

We are given the rule `Controller`, so remember that you are going to need a class `Controller` in your Python code. The second line is:

label_wid: my_custom_label

This code line gives defines the label for this rule from a reference to the `Label`. The third line is:

BoxLayout:

We start the definition of the properties for the layout. In the fourth and fifth lines:

orientation: 'horizontal'
padding: 20

We give values to the properties: in this case, horizontal to the orientation and *20* to the padding (the empty space beyond the border of the window). The sixth, seventh, and eighth lines are:

```
Button:
    text: 'My controller info is: ' + root.info
    on_press: root.do_action()
```

This is the definition for the button. Here is the most important part of the designing with the Kv language: the order in which it appears in the code is the same as that in which the widgets are arranged in the layout, so the button will be the leftmost of all the widgets that we will use. The final part of the code is the definition of the `Label`:

```
Label:
    id: my_custom_label
    text: 'My label before button press'
```

There's more...

An interesting modification can be done to the following fourth line of the KV file:

```
orientation: 'horizontal'
```

To change the orientation of `BoxLayout` from horizontal to vertical, we can change the preceding line to the following line:

```
orientation: 'vertical'
```

It will have the same functionality, but the button will be above the label.

See also

If you want more details about widgets and layouts, see the recipes in *Chapter 4, Widgets*.

Running your code

In this recipe, we want to teach you how to run the code that we have constructed using the Kivy framework.

Getting ready

This recipe needs some code to be run and Kivy to be properly installed. We will use the code in the recipe *Relating Python code and the Kv language,* where we have two files, `e4.kv` and `e4.py`.

How to do it...

This recipe may seem easy because it is just a few steps, but the explanation is important. Use Python from the shell to run the file e4.py:

```
$ Python e4.py --size=250x200
```

It will display:

How it works...

As we've already seen in the recipe *Relating Python code and the Kv language*, the call to the e4.kv file occurs inside the e4.py code; as such, Kivy does not need an explicit reference. We used the option size previously because Kivy has a default size (usually *800x600 pixels*) that did not meet our expectations.

There's more...

Well, if you are using a different operative system, there are some other considerations.

Mac OS X

With Mac OS X we use a portable package and we need to run the file a little bit differently:

```
$ kivy e4.py --size=250x200
```

This is because the Kivy framework has been packed with Python in the program call `kivy`.

Microsoft Windows

In Microsoft Windows, the portable package is called with a secondary click, using **Send to** menu, and selecting **Kivy**.

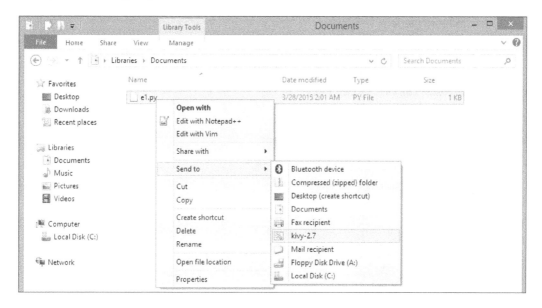

See also

If you are interested in how to run your code on a mobile device, go to *Chapter 9, Kivy for Mobile Devices*.

Using Kivy garden

This recipe will teach you how to use Kivy garden, which is a helpful tool to get some Kivy add-ons.

Getting ready

This recipe needs the `pip` system, which is a package management system used to install and manage software packages written in Python. The installation is very easy: just go to `https://pip.pypa.io/en/latest/installing.html` and download `get-pip.py`. Now, in the terminal, type:

```
$ Python get-pip.py
```

This line installs `pip`.

How to do it...

These are the most important tasks with Kivy garden:

1. Install Kivy garden:

    ```
    $ sudo pip install kivy-garden
    ```

2. Install a garden package:

    ```
    $ garden install graph
    ```

3. Upgrade a garden package:

    ```
    $ garden install --upgrade graph
    ```

4. Uninstall a garden package:

    ```
    $ garden uninstall graph
    ```

5. List all the garden packages installed:

    ```
    $ garden list
    ```

There's more...

Also, we want to be able to search in the Kivy garden; for example, we can:

1. Search new packages:

    ```
    $ garden search
    ```

2. Search all the packages that contain graph:

    ```
    $ garden search graph
    ```

3. Show the following:

    ```
    $ garden --help
    ```

    All the garden packages are installed by default in `~/.kivy/garden`.

Packing

If you want to include garden packages in your application, you can add the app to the `install` command. This will create a `libs/garden` directory in your current directory, which will be used by Kivy garden.

For example in my app, it is in the directory `MyApp`:

```
$ cd myapp
$ garden install --app graph
```

2
Input, Motion, and Touch

In this chapter, we will cover:

- ▸ Using the mouse
- ▸ Evolving to the touchscreen
- ▸ Working with the accelerometer
- ▸ Using the gyroscope
- ▸ The Differences between the touch and motion events
- ▸ Recognizing touch shapes
- ▸ Detecting multitapping
- ▸ Grabbing touch events
- ▸ Recording gestures

Introduction

The Kivy framework is able to handle most common types of input and actions such as mouse, touchscreen, accelerometer, and gyroscope that will be reviewed in this chapter. It handles the native multitouch protocols on the following platforms: Tuio, WM_Touch, MacMultitouchSupport, MT Protocol A/B, and Android.

The class of all input events is **motion event**. It generates two kinds of events; one of them is **touch events**—a motion event that contains at least an x and y position. All the touch events are dispatched across the widget tree. The **no-touch events** are the rest. The accelerometer is a continuous event, without position. It never starts or stops. These events are not dispatched across the widget tree.

Using the mouse

This recipe will teach you how to use the first kind of input, probably the most used, the mouse. We will consider the mouse input as a touch event, so the (x, y) position of the touch (0-1 range) will be scaled to the window size (width/height) and dispatched to the following:

- **on_touch_down**: An event is fired when a touch down event is initiated. Subsequently, the respective widget's on_touch_down() method is called.

- **on_touch_move**: An event is fired when a touch event moves (changes location). Subsequently, the respective widget's on_touch_move() method is called.

- **on_touch_up**: An event is fired when a down event is released (terminated). Subsequently, the respective widget's on_touch_up() method is called.

Getting ready

In this recipe, we will use the Kv language for the design of the widgets, so you will need to be familiar with the language or have completed the previous chapter. Also, this recipe will use the common Button widget for reference.

How to do it...

Follow the steps in this recipe:

1. First, let's start with the KV file:

```
<MyW>:
    Button:
        id: button1
        text: 'Hello'
```

In the class of the widget in the Python code, we need to override the method on_touch_down because the method is already defined in the Kivy framework.

2. Change the button text with the information in touch.button:

```
import kivy
kivy.require('1.9.0')

from kivy.app import App
from kivy.uix.widget import Widget

class MyW(Widget):

    def on_touch_down(self, touch):
        if 'button' in touch.profile:
```

```
            self.ids.button1.text = touch.button

    class e1App(App):

        def build(self):
            return MyW()

    if __name__ == '__main__':
        e1App().run()
```

How it works...

Let's start with the KV file. The first line is the name of the rule, similar to the class name in the Python file. The second line is the definition of the button widget, and the third line is the ID of the button, which is necessary to do the call of the widget inside the Python code, and the fourth line is the definition of the text in the button.

With regard to the Python code, the initial four lines are usual to use Kivy and the button widget. Note the following fifth line:

```
class MyW(Widget):
```

This is where we define the class associated with our rule in the KV file. Now consider the sixth line:

```
def on_touch_down(self, touch):
```

Here, we start the declaration of the dispatched on_touch_down method; you must note the parameter touch in the declaration, and this parameter is necessary to call the event using the input—in this case—the mouse. Next, the seventh line is:

```
if 'button' in touch.profile:
```

This is a verification line, because we need to be sure that the input device used in the platform, where we are running our code, supports the button profile. If this line is not present when the next line is performed, the app could crash. Finally, the eighth line:

```
self.ids.button1.text = touch.button
```

This line is where we do the call to the button profile, which gives the information on which mouse button is touched by the user (the right one, left one, scroll up, and so on). Using this information, we change the text in our button that has ID button1. The last lines of the Python code are usual to run and display our Kivy interface. Just remember that the initial part of the name of the classis as follows:

```
class e1App(App):
```

Note that it will be the same as the KV file, so the name of the KV file in this case is `e1.kv`.

A last thing to remark is that we do not limit the input event to the button, so the touch can occur anywhere within the window.

There's more...

Another interesting profile that we could call for the mouse is the `pos` attribute, which provides us with the position vector of the click in the window. Let's change the seventh line of the Python code to:

```
self.ids.button1.text = str(touch.pos)
```

When we are calling the `pos` profile and changing the text in the button widget to the position where the click is performed, the `str()` built-in object is important because the `touch.pos` return is a vector. This means that we need to convert to a string to avoid compatibility issues.

See also

If you want to run your interface, take a look at our recipe *Running your code*. To get further details about widgets, see the recipes in *Chapter 4, Widgets*.

Evolving to the touchscreen

In this recipe, we are evolving to the touchscreen. Here, you will see the basic differences between the mouse and the touchscreen. This will give us more options than with the mouse device.

Getting ready

For this recipe, we will use the Kv language for the design of the widgets, so make sure that you are confident with it and refresh your knowledge if necessary. Also, this recipe will use the common button and label widgets for reference. Obviously, to get more benefit, a touchscreen device is useful to run the code.

How to do it...

Perform the following steps:

1. In the KV file, declare the button and the label:

   ```
   <MyW>:
       Button:
           id: button1
   ```

```
            text: 'Hello'
        Label:
            id: label1
            pos: 100, 100
            text: 'My label before press the screen'
```

2. In the class of the widget in the Python code, we need to override the method `on_touch_down`

3. Change the button text with the information in `touch.button`

4. Change the label text with the information in `touch.pressure`

```
import kivy
kivy.require('1.9.0')

from kivy.app import App
from kivy.uix.widget import Widget

class MyW(Widget):

    def on_touch_down(self, touch):
        if 'button' in touch.profile:
            self.ids.button1.text = touch.button

        if 'pressure' in touch.profile:
            self.ids.label1.text =\
            str(touch.pressure)

class e2App(App):

    def build(self):
        return MyW()

if __name__ == '__main__':
    e2App().run()
```

How it works...

Well, let's first review the KV file. The first line is the name of the rule, the same as of the class in the Python file. The second line is the definition of the button widget, the third line is the ID of the button, which is necessary to do the call of the widget inside the Python code, and the fourth line is the definition of the text in the button. The fifth line is the definition of the label widget. The sixth line is where we give the ID to the label, the seventh line is where we give the position to the label. I should point out that the button is using the default position (0, 0), so we will have to give a different position to the label widget to avoid overlapping. The eight is the definition of the initial text in the label.

With regard to the Python code, the initial four lines are usual to use Kivy and the widgets. Note the fifth one:

```
class MyW(Widget):
```

This is where we define the class associated with our rule in the KV file. The sixth line:

```
def on_touch_down(self, touch):
```

Here, we start the declaration of the dispatched `on_touch_down` method. You must note the parameter touch in the declaration as this parameter is necessary to call the event, which is done by the input (in this case, the mouse). The seventh line is:

```
if 'button' in touch.profile:
```

It is a verification line because we need to be sure that the input device used in the platform, where we are running our code, supports the button profile. If this line is not present when the next one is performed, the app could crash. The eighth line is:

```
self.ids.button1.text = touch.button
```

This line is where we do the call to the profile button, which gives the information of what button is touched by the user (the right, left, scroll up button, and so on) and we changed the text in the button with the ID `button1` with that information. The ninth line is:

```
if 'pressure' in touch.profile:
```

This is the other verification line and is important because, due to the fact that pressure is specific to some touchscreen devices, it is necessary to avoid crashes. The tenth and eleventh line:

```
self.ids.label1.text =\
str(touch.pressure)
```

Those lines are where we change the text of the label to the pressure value of the specific touch.

The last lines of the Python code are usual to run and display our Kivy interface. Just remember that the initial part of the name of the class is:

```
class e2App(App):
```

It will be the same in relation to the KV file. For example, the name of the KV file in this case is `e2.kv`.

The final thing to remark is that we do not limit the input event to the button, so the touch can occur anywhere within the window or the screen.

There's more...

Actually, your device could have more profiles than we saw in this recipe. Let's change the code to know that for your specific device. Remove the ninth line and change the tenth and eleventh lines to:

```
self.ids.label1.text =\
str(touch.profile)
```

These lines will change the label's text for all the profiles available for your device. Thus, you can get more yield of your app.

See also

If you want to run your interface, take a look at our recipe Running your code, and to get more detail about widgets, see the recipes in *Chapter 4*, *Widgets*. If you want to run the code in a mobile device, see *Chapter 9*, *Kivy for Mobile Devices*.

Working with the accelerometer

Nowadays, it is common that mobile devices are equipped with an accelerometer. Thereby, it is relevant to consider this input to develop fancy apps. The accelerometer is one kind of event that is considered as a no-touch event because it has neither start nor an end, it is always providing information.

Getting ready

In this recipe, we will use the Kv language for the design of the widgets, so, again, you will need to be familiar with the Kv language. Also, this recipe will use the common button and label widgets for reference. Obviously, to get more benefit, a device with an accelerometer is useful to run the code.

It is necessary to install a package for the use of the accelerometer in any mobile device; there is a way to deal with every specific device, but we do not have to reinvent the wheel. Let's use a `Plyer` package, which is an effort from many of the Kivy developers. To install the package from the shell, use:

```
$ sudo pip plyer install
```

Here where we are using `pip` to install the `Plyer` package, if you do not have `pip` installed in your computer, see the recipe *Using Kivy Garden* in *Chapter 1*, *Kivy and the Kv language*.

How to do it...

To complete this recipe, follow these steps:

1. In the KV file, define the four labels and the button:

```
<Accel>:
    Label:
        id: label1
        pos: 150, 300
        text: 'X: '

    Label:
        id: label2
        pos: 150, 250
        text: 'Y: '

    Label:
        id: label3
        pos: 150, 200
        text: 'Z: '

    Label:
        id: status
        pos: 150, 150
        text: ''

    Button:
        id: button1
        pos: 150, 50
        text: 'Start'
        on_press: root.pressed1()
```

2. In the Python file, import the usual packages to use Kivys.

3. Import the `Clock` and `Plyer` packages.

4. In the class for the rule, define a class to standby the accelerometer.

5. Define the method to start to retrieve data from the accelerometer.

6. Define the method when the button is pressed:

```
from kivy.app import App
from kivy.properties import ObjectProperty
from kivy.uix.widget import Widget
```

```python
from kivy.clock import Clock
from plyer import accelerometer

class Accel(Widget):
    def __init__(self):
        super(Accel, self).__init__()
        self.sensorEnabled = False

    def get_acceleration(self, dt):
        val = accelerometer.acceleration

        self.ids.label1.text = "X: " + str(val[0])
        self.ids.label2.text = "Y: " + str(val[1])
        self.ids.label3.text = "Z: " + str(val[2])

    def pressed1(self):
        try:
            if not self.sensorEnabled:
                accelerometer.enable()
                Clock.schedule_interval(self.get_acceleration,
                1 / 20.)

                self.sensorEnabled = True
                self.ids.button1.text = "Stop"
            else:
                accelerometer.disable()
                Clock.unschedule(self.get_acceleration)

                self.sensorEnabled = False
                self.ids.button1.text = "Start"
        except NotImplementedError:
            import traceback; traceback.print_exc()
            self.ids.status.text =\
"Accelerometer is not supported for your   platform"

class e3App(App):
    def build(self):
        return Accel()

if __name__ == '__main__':
    e3App().run()
```

How it works...

First, review the KV file. Note that the first line is the name of the rule, similar to the class in the Python file. Included in the next lines are the definitions of the four labels that we will use, so note the text of the label with the ID status. It will likely be blank, but it will be visible only when we modify this field from the Python code.

In the Python code, the first three lines are usual to import `kivy` and the widgets. The fourth line:

```
from kivy.clock import Clock
```

This will import the clock, which is used to get the accelerometer value in a time lap because, as we already said, this input is continuously providing data. The fifth line:

```
from plyer import accelerometer
```

This is importing the package `plyer`, which is the one that makes it possible to retrieve the data from an iOS or Android device. The sixth line:

```
class Accel(Widget):
```

This is the line where the class for the rule starts. Its name must be the same as the Kivy rule. The seventh, eighth, and ninth lines are:

```
    def __init__(self):
        super(Accel, self).__init__()
        self.sensorEnabled = False
```

These define the method that initializes the class and put in standby the accelerometer to be used later. The tenth, eleventh, twelfth, thirteenth, and fourteenth lines are:

```
    def get_acceleration(self, dt):
        val = accelerometer.acceleration
        self.ids.label1.text = "X: " + str(val[0])
        self.ids.label2.text = "Y: " + str(val[1])
        self.ids.label3.text = "Z: " + str(val[2])
```

These lines are used to retrieve the data of the accelerometer and will modify the text of the first three labels with the data of the acceleration. Now, look at the fifteenth line:

```
    def pressed1(self):
```

This is where we define the method performed when the button is pressed. In the sixteenth line, we start a `try` sentence to start getting data from the accelerometer. In the seventeenth line, it is shown that if the accelerometer is disabled, enable it or vice versa. The eighteenth line is:

```
Clock.schedule_interval(self.get_acceleration, 1 / 20.)
```

In this line, we do the acquisition of the acceleration in time intervals. The acceleration is acquired by calling the `get_acceleration` method. The next class is usual to display our Kivy interface.

There's more...

Also, the `plyer` package allows you to interact with the compass and the GPS of the mobile device using a similar procedure. In the case of the compass, it is very easy to change. The change in the code is the word `gyroscope` for `compass` and `acceleration` for `orientation`.

See also

To get more details about widgets, see the recipes in *Chapter 4*, *Widgets*, and if you want to run the code in a mobile device, see *Chapter 9*, *Kivy for Mobile Devices*.

Using the gyroscope

Mobile devices today also have a gyroscope. The gyroscope is considered as a no-touch event. This kind of event does not have a start or an end; it is always providing information.

Getting ready

For this recipe, we will use the Kv language for the design of the widgets. Also, this recipe will use the common button and label widgets for reference. Obviously, to run the code of this recipe properly, a device with a gyroscope is necessary.

It is necessary to install a package to use the gyroscope with any mobile device. While there is a way to deal with specific devices, we do not have to reinvent the wheel. Let's use the `plyer` package, which is an effort from many of the Kivy developers. To install the package from the shell, use:

```
$ sudo pip plyer install
```

How to do it...

To complete this recipe, follow these steps:

1. In the KV file, define the four labels and the button:

```
<Acce>:
    Label:
        id: label1
        pos: 150, 300
```

```
            text: 'X: '

    Label:
        id: label2
        pos: 150, 250
        text: 'Y: '

    Label:
        id: label3
        pos: 150, 200
        text: 'Z: '

    Label:
        id: status
        pos: 150, 150
        text: ''

    Button:
        id: button1
        pos: 150, 50
        text: 'Start'
        on_press: root.pressed1()
```

2. In the Python file, import the usual packages to use Kivy.

3. Import the `Clock` and `plyer` packages.

4. In the class for the rule, define a class to stand by the gyroscope.

5. Define the method to start to retrieve data from the gyroscope.

6. Define the method when the button is pressed:

```python
from kivy.app import App
from kivy.properties import ObjectProperty
from kivy.uix.widget import Widget

from kivy.clock import Clock
from plyer import gyroscope

class Acce(Widget):
    def __init__(self):
        super(Acce, self).__init__()
        self.sensorEnabled = False

    def get_orientation(self, dt):
        val = gyroscope.orientation
```

```
                self.ids.label1.text = "X: " + str(val[0])
                self.ids.label2.text = "Y: " + str(val[1])
                self.ids.label3.text = "Z: " + str(val[2])

        def pressed1(self):
            try:
                if not self.sensorEnabled:
                    gyroscope.enable()
                    Clock.schedule_interval(self.get_orientation,
                    1 / 20.)

                    self.sensorEnabled = True
                    self.ids.button1.text = "Stop"
                else:
                    gyroscope.disable()
                    Clock.unschedule(self.get_orientation)

                    self.sensorEnabled = False
                    self.ids.button1.text = "Start"
            except NotImplementedError:
                import traceback; traceback.print_exc()
                self.ids.status.text =\
    "Gyroscope is not supported for your   platform"

class e4App(App):
    def build(self):
        return Acce()

if __name__ == '__main__':
    e4App().run()
```

How it works...

The KV file that we are using is similar to the last recipe's KV file. We define four labels and the start button.

In the Python code, the first three lines are usual to import `kivy` and the widgets. The fourth line:

```
from kivy.clock import Clock
```

We are importing the clock, which is used to get the accelerometer value in a time lap because, as we already said, this input is continuously providing data. The fifth line:

```
from plyer import gyroscope
```

This is importing the package `plyer`, which is the one that makes it possible to retrieve the data from an iOS or Android device. The sixth line:

```
class Acce(Widget):
```

It is the line where the class for the rule starts and its name must be the same as in the Kivy rule. The seventh, eighth, and ninth lines are:

```
def __init__(self):
    super(Acce, self).__init__()
    self.sensorEnabled = False
```

Those are where we define the methods that initialize the class and put the accelerometer on standby to be used later. The tenth, eleventh, twelfth, thirteenth, and fourteenth lines are as follows:

```
def get_orientation(self, dt):
    val = gyroscope.orientation
    self.ids.label1.text = "X: " + str(val[0])
    self.ids.label2.text = "Y: " + str(val[1])
    self.ids.label3.text = "Z: " + str(val[2])
```

Those lines are allowing us to retrieve data from the gyroscope and enabling us to modify the text of the first three labels with the data of the orientation. The fifteenth line:

```
def pressed1(self):
```

It is where we define the method performed when the button is pressed. In the sixteenth line, we start a `try` sentence to start to get data from the gyroscope. With the seventeenth line, we can open an `if` sentence for the case that the gyroscope is unable, enable it. The eighteenth line:

```
Clock.schedule_interval(self.get_orientation, 1 / 20.)
```

In this line, we can get the intervals of the orientation by calling the `get_orientation` method. The next class is the usual one to display our Kivy interface.

See also

If you want to run the code in a mobile device, see *Chapter 9*, *Kivy for Mobile Devices*.

The differences between the touch and motion events

There is a key difference between touch and motion events. A motion event is a continuous succession of many touch events. However, we also know that a touch event always has the pos profile, namely **position information**. The motion event, however, is not dispatched throughout the widget tree.

Getting ready

In this recipe, we will use the Kv language for the design of the widgets, so we assume that the reader is familiar with the Kv language or did the lecture of the first chapter. Also, this recipe will use the common button widget for reference.

How to do it...

Use this recipe and follow these steps:

1. First, in the KV file, define a button:

```
<MyW>:
    Button:
        id: button1
        pos: 0,0
        text: 'Hello'
```

2. In the class of the widget in the Python code, we need to override the method on_touch_move.

3. Change the button's position with the information in touch.pos:

```
import kivy
kivy.require('1.9.0')

from kivy.app import App
from kivy.uix.widget import Widget

class MyW(Widget):

    def on_touch_move(self, touch):
        if 'pos' in touch.profile:
            self.ids.button1.pos = touch.pos

class e5App(App):
```

```
        def build(self):
            return MyW()

    if __name__ == '__main__':
        e5App().run()
```

How it works...

Let's start with the KV file, the first line is the name of the rule, similar to the class in the Python file. The second line is the definition of the button widget, the third line is the ID of the button, which is necessary to do the call of the widget inside the Python code, the fourth line specifies the initial position of the button, and the fifth line is the definition of the text in the button.

In the Python code, the initial four lines are usual to use Kivy and the button widget. The fifth one:

```
class MyW(Widget):
```

It is where we define the class associated with our rule in the KV file. The sixth line:

```
def on_touch_move(self, touch):
```

Here, we start the declaration of the dispatched `on_touch_move` method; you must note the parameter touch in the declaration, as this parameter is necessary to call the event using the input. Now the seventh line:

```
if 'pos' in touch.profile:
```

This is a verification line, because we need to be sure that the input device used in the platform, where we are running our code, supports the button profile. If this line is not present when the next one is performed, the app could crash. The eighth line:

```
self.ids.button1.pos = touch.pos
```

This line is where we do the call to the profile position, which gives the information of where the touch occurs, and we changed the position of the button with the ID `button1` with that information. The last lines of the Python code are usual to run and display our Kivy interface. Just remember that the initial part of the name of the class is:

```
class e5App(App):
```

It will be same as the KV file; the name of the KV file in this case is `e5.kv`.

The last thing to remark is that we do not limit the input event to the button, so the touch can occur anywhere in the window.

There's more...

Also, the motion events are compatible with the touch event. It is possible to add to our code to the class `MyW` a `on_touch_down` method like this:

```
def on_touch_down(self, touch):
    if 'button' in touch.profile:
        self.ids.button1.text = touch.button
```

With this addition, now when you touch the text inside, the button is going to change to the information about which button is used.

See also

To get more details about widgets, see the recipes in *Chapter 4, Widgets*.

Recognizing touch shapes

There is a useful tool provided by Kivy that permits us to recognize the shape of the touch that is performed. In this recipe, we will go through the foundations of using it.

Getting ready

In this recipe, we will use the Kv language for the design of the widgets, so we assume that the reader is familiar with the Kv language. Also, this recipe will use the common button and label widgets for reference.

How to do it...

Follow these steps:

1. First, in the KV file, define a button and an empty label:

```
<MyW>:
    Button:
        id: button1
        pos: 0,0
        text: 'Hello'

    Label:
        id: label1
        pos: 50, 200
        text: ''
```

2. In the class of the widget in the Python code, we need to override the method `on_touch_move`.

3. Change the button position to the information in `touch.pos`.

4. Change the text in the label when a rectangular shape is present:

```python
import kivy
kivy.require('1.9.0')

from kivy.app import App
from kivy.uix.widget import Widget
from kivy.input.shape import ShapeRect

class MyW(Widget):

    def on_touch_move(self, touch):
        if 'pos' in touch.profile:
            self.ids.button1.pos = touch.pos
        if isinstance(touch.shape, ShapeRect):
            self.ids.label1.text =\
'My touch have a rectangle shape of size' + str(touch.shape.
width)+ str(touch.shape.height)

class e6App(App):

    def build(self):
        return MyW()

if __name__ == '__main__':
    e6App().run()
```

How it works...

In the KV file, the first line as usual is the name of the rule. The second line is the definition of the button widget, the third line is the ID of the button, which is necessary to do the call of the widget inside the Python code, the fourth line specifies the initial position of the button, and the fifth line is the definition of the text in the button. The sixth line is the definition of the label widget, the seventh line is ID of the label, the eighth line is the initial position of the label, and the ninth line is the initial text of the label.

In relation to the Python code, the initial four lines are the usual lines to use Kivy and the button widget. Next, the fifth one:

```python
from kivy.input.shape import ShapeRect
```

In this line, we import the information of `ShapeRect` to be compared with the touch performed in the app. The sixth line is:

```
class MyW(Widget):
```

This is where we define the class associated with our rule in the KV file. The seventh line:

```
def on_touch_move(self, touch):
```

Here, we start the declaration of the dispatched `on_touch_move` method; you must note the parameter touch in the declaration, and this parameter is necessary to call the event by the input. The eighth and ninth lines are:

```
if 'pos' in touch.profile:
    self.ids.button1.pos = touch.pos
```

Those lines change the position of the button. The tenth line is:

```
if isinstance(touch.shape, ShapeRect):
```

It is where the comparison between the imported shape and the shape of the touch is performed. The eleventh line will change the label text with the dimension of the touch if this is rectangular. The last lines of the Python code are the usual lines to run and display our Kivy interface. Just remember that the initial part of the name of the class is:

```
class e6App(App):
```

It will be the same of the KV file; the name of the KV file in this case is `e6.kv`

See also

If you want to run your interface, take a look at our recipe *Running your code*, and to get more details about widgets, see the recipes in *Chapter 4*, *Widgets*.

Detecting multitapping

The multitapping detection is a useful tool in the development of an app. When more than a touch occurs in a zone, it is what we call a **multitap**.

Getting ready

We will work with the `on_touch_down` method, so it could be useful to go through the recipe *Evolving to the touchscreen* in this chapter. Also, this recipe will use the common button and label widgets for reference.

How to do it...

Follow these steps in this recipe:

1. First, in the KV file, define a button and an empty label:

```
<MyW>:
    Button:
        id: button1
        pos: 0,0
        text: 'Hello'

    Label:
        id: label1
        pos: 200, 200
        text: ''
```

2. In the class of the widget in the Python code, we need to override the method on_touch_down.

3. Change the text in the label when a double tap is present.

4. Change the text in the label when a triple tap is present:

```
import kivy
kivy.require('1.9.0')

from kivy.app import App
from kivy.uix.widget import Widget

class MyW(Widget):

    def on_touch_down(self, touch):
        if touch.is_double_tap:
            self.ids.label1.text = 'Touch is a double tap !
            - The interval is: '+
            str(touch.double_tap_time)
        elif touch.is_triple_tap:
            self.ids.label1.text = "Touch is a triple tap !
            - The interval is: {0} \nand distance between
            previous is {1}".format(touch.triple_tap_time,
            touch.triple_tap_distance)

class e7App(App):
    def build(self):
        return MyW()

if __name__ == '__main__':
    e7App().run()
```

How it works...

We are again using our KV file with a simple button and empty label with the ID `button1` and `label1` respectively.

In the Python code, the initial four lines are usual to use Kivy and the button widget. The fifth line is:

```
class MyW(Widget):
```

It is where we define the class associated with our rule in the KV file. The sixth line is:

```
def on_touch_down(self, touch):
```

Here, we start the declaration of the dispatched `on_touch_down` method; you must note the parameter touch in the declaration and this parameter is necessary to call the event by the input. The seventh and eighth lines are:

```
if touch.is_double_tap:
self.ids.label1.text = 'Touch is a double tap ! - The
interval is: '+ str(touch.double_tap_time)
```

These lines are where we detect if the tap is double. If it is true, we change the text of the label defined in the KV file with the string `Touch is a double tap! - The interval is:` plus the time that the double tap takes. The ninth and tenth lines:

```
        elif touch.is_triple_tap:
self.ids.label1.text = "Touch is a triple tap ! - The
interval is: {0} \nand distance between previous is
{1}".format(touch.triple_tap_time, touch.triple_tap_distance)
```

Those lines change the text of the label if the touch in a triple tab. The last lines of the Python code are the usual lines to run and display our Kivy interface. Just remember that the initial part of the name of the class is:

```
class e7App(App):
```

It will be similar to the KV file; the name of the KV file in this case is `e7.kv`.

Grabbing touch events

There are some moments or areas where we do not want the touch performed in the same way. Therefore, we can grab some inputs to give them special treatment.

Getting ready

We will continue working with the touch profile, so it could be useful to review the previous recipes for a deeper understanding, also we will use the same KV file with the common button and label widgets whereby you will find a detailed explanation of the KV file in the recipe *Recognizing touch shapes*.

How to do it...

This recipe following the next steps:

1. In the KV file, define a button and a empty label:

```
<MyW>:
    Button:
        id: button1
        pos: 0,0
        text: 'Hello'

    Label:
        id: label1
        pos: 200, 200
        text: ''
```

2. In the class of the widget in the Python code, we need to override the method on_touch_down.

3. If the touch coincides with the button area, grab the touch.

4. In the class of the widget in the Python code, we also need to override the method on_touch_up.

5. If the touch is grabbed, change the text of the label and ungrab the touch.

6. Otherwise change the text of the label of that of a different text:

```
import kivy
kivy.require('1.9.0')

from kivy.app import App
from kivy.uix.widget import Widget

class MyW(Widget):

    def on_touch_down(self, touch):
        if self.ids.button1.collide_point(*touch.pos):
            touch.grab(self)
            return True

    def on_touch_up(self, touch):
```

```
        if touch.grab_current is self:

            self.ids.label1.text =\
'Click on the screen but over the Button'
            touch.ungrab(self)
            return True
        else:
            self.ids.label1.text =\
'Click on the screen'

class e8App(App):

    def build(self):
        return MyW()

if __name__ == '__main__':
    e8App().run()
```

How it works...

Again, in the KV file, we have the definition of a button and a empty label.

In the Python code, the initial four lines are the usual lines to use Kivy and the button widget. The fifth line is:

```
class MyW(Widget):
```

This is where we define the class associated with our rule in the KV file. The sixth line is:

```
def on_touch_down(self, touch):
```

Here, we start the declaration of the dispatched on_touch_down method; you must note the parameter touch in the declaration and this parameter is necessary to call the event do it by the input. The seventh, eighth, and ninth lines are:

```
        if self.ids.button1.collide_point(*touch.pos):
            touch.grab(self)
            return True
```

In these lines, we check whether the touch falls in the area of the button, and if so, we grab the touch. In the tenth line, we define the dispatched on_touch_up to make the decision of what to do with the grabbed touch. In the eleventh line, there is the if statement where if the touch is grabbed, we change the label to the text 'Click on the screen but over the Button' In the thirteen line, we ungrab the touch:

```
touch.ungrab(self)
```

In the fifteenth line, we have the `else` statement where we change the text of the label to `'Click on the screen'`. This section is optional, but you're strongly encouraged to include it and your editor may want to discuss with you why you have not.

The last lines of the Python code are the usual lines to run and display our Kivy interface. Just remember that the initial part of the name of the class is:

```
class e8App(App):
```

It will be the same as the KV file; the name of the KV file in this case is `e8.kv`.

Recording gestures

A gesture is a particular succession of touches, which we will give some special significance to. Kivy eases the way to handle gestures.

Getting ready

In this recipe, we will use some predefined graphics in the Kivy framework just to highlight the gesture, and you do not need any further knowledge about it. Also, we have a predefined gesture that is provided in this recipe to you.

How to do it...

In this recipe, we have the next steps:

1. Call the gesture database.
2. Make a method to categorize the gesture.
3. Set a marker for the initial touch.
4. Record the touch.
5. Do the comparison with the predefined gesture.
6. Print the result:

   ```python
   from kivy.app import App

   from kivy.uix.widget import Widget
   from kivy.uix.button import Button
   from kivy.graphics import Color, Ellipse, Line
   from kivy.gesture import Gesture, GestureDatabase

   gdb = GestureDatabase()

   check =\ gdb.str_to_gesture('eNq1l0tuI0cMhvd9EXsTofgmL6BsA/
   ```

```
gAgcYWb\GMmtmBpksztwyY1kgZI0rNpbdr+u+pjkX+9+v718+uf3zbP++Pp68d++
v\X8PIzp/ukA08Pd2+6P/d10wPwzHzQdH+6Op4/3z/tj/svT/ZeDTPf/Cnm\
oZtNBZ5Rl/8P769tp7uZzt/iPbr/NraYD9AjmIXzLLoDTdmxgBLsSMMIw\5OHzcP6e
X9O0/WVsCMFGmCuaGgjBdPy0+/8wXGFkeu4Ig7LzgISbMw/j6\fh8hmMMMBDIkdBY
PimV4pQ7W8EQMUA4LMhMzCyW5watKgJoOHhxsuIz3ws\cVb8ExhpIxDoIgvcEzhoai
Z1geA20Rj+UAwlp4LDxd8OkqO4KHYXLI4oY\OwEai4oPRmHiZXr6iXOiY9mXBFUNYa
cAVDm4uIOCiaXws24plK9oq7PIU\r56iOqsyg+acyOrezJicpTCI3YYy5HtapFNZSl
dLCcRgCCk4hqniDZ2dH\ZjCMf1EXh47laNEN2MfEjkzJFgtK3BLHwEAGTcnlSu7LNP
LUbo6+n2m5G\bAuVzUr/ShYQzoSBSWi5iXJwyVqWRr4ctX+om1mq+GR7ibAA8dJuHL
fC5\nGVbjl7dMS/tk1g3tB3OXZyWXsyyrsMtWtlXY5SnHGmwpPwW+s3M15h5C\
kVvM8FyWcWH3Uce5io00A/8Eu7wUWoVdXoqswi4v5eIlseTWl6e9Cqh6+\
IUt6OoUwAJD88KwjC4rJVZAazmpsAa6jFRaA10+qqyBLht1DRu1bNQ1bL\
Sy0S425mWFOc9khtxcnRwuaEW6PZnH8sFp5aPRKuwy0i5GMnsmHJE32dz\
73a5oG3nJgLyemqDgXKtPu/m2//ix379d7u6m8+XdbLrf5jg2Y9picD5O\B/NpN4v
QIrYYLWKJHiX6aJFblBahRSvRvEUsETuQjRapxe6uHSjPsBK7u\0CL0mKUyLKJ25/
NLbRaUI+PzwGsRWrxzOr0qKNy5+ydHnVUzsftj7JFdK\7cAUSrW3SugrdpReeqdlu
V6Fxdu6hdv6hcCeYabQl7KFG5ElWpiM6itqg\tWovWorXYlU6/d234y/71+eWUVud1
dRvz2xT/en06vcwfWiP7QFU51dP7\l/3H7u1xX2+gP9F+/MHc7jw1fz98vD99fTx
V65yN6YfP81jE8nDMa8j81\bD5B2R9zCo=')
```

```python
def simplegesture(name, point_list):
    g = Gesture()
    g.add_stroke(point_list)
    g.normalize()
    g.name = name
    return g


class GestureBoard(Widget):

    def __init__(self, *args, **kwargs):
        super(GestureBoard, self).__init__()
        self.gdb = GestureDatabase()
        self.gdb.add_gesture(check)

    def on_touch_down(self, touch):
        userdata = touch.ud
        with self.canvas:
            Color(1, 1, 0)
            d = 30.0
            Ellipse(pos=(touch.x - d/2, touch.y - d/2),
            size=(d, d)) userdata['line'] =
            Line(points=(touch.x, touch.y))
        return True

    def on_touch_move(self, touch):
        try:
```

```
                    touch.ud['line'].points += [touch.x, touch.y]
                    return True
                except (KeyError) as e:
                    pass

        def on_touch_up(self, touch):
            g = simplegesture('',list(zip(touch.ud['line'].
            points[::2],touch.ud['line'].points[1::2])))
    print("gesture representation:",self.gdb.gesture_to_str(g))
            print("check:", g.get_score(check))
            g2 = self.gdb.find(g, minscore=0.70)
            print(g2)
            if g2:
                if g2[1] == check: print("check")
            self.canvas.clear()

    class e9App(App):
        def build(self):
            return GestureBoard()

    if __name__ == '__main__':
        e9App().run()
```

How It works...

As usual, the first three lines are to use Kivy and the widgets. The fourth line is where we import predefined graphics to later represent the start of the gesture. In the fifth line, we import the gesture profile and the database structure. In the sixth line, we initialize the gesture database. The seventh line is read from the terminal using a code like this for a gesture with the figure of a check (check mark). Next, we define the method simplegesture:

```
    def simplegesture(name, point_list):
        g = Gesture()
        g.add_stroke(point_list)
        g.normalize()
        g.name = name
        return g
```

This method returns a gesture from a list of points. In the class of the widget, we define the initial method where we start the gesture database and we add the check gesture. In the `on_touch_down` definition, we put a circle in the first touch and added this position to the list of touches. In the `on_touch_move` method we added the rest of the points of the gesture to the list of touches. In the `on_touch_up` method, which is triggered when the gesture is released, we convert the list of touches to a gesture using the method `simplegesture`. Also in this method, we have the line:

```
g2 = self.gdb.find(g, minscore=0.70)
```

In the preceding line, we evaluate if the gesture is the gesture database with a 70 percent tolerance and we print the result with the next lines in the terminal.

There's more...

Now, you have a way to record a gesture and you can feed the gesture database with different gestures. An important recommendation to do this is to separate the predefined gestures in to another file, which will contain only this information.

See also

To get more details about widgets, see the recipes in *Chapter 4, Widgets,* and for graphics, see *Chapter 5, Graphics – Canvas and Instructions.*

3
Events

In this chapter, we will cover:

- ▶ Scheduling a one-time event
- ▶ Scheduling a repetitive event
- ▶ Triggering events
- ▶ Defining widget events
- ▶ Creating custom events
- ▶ Attaching callbacks
- ▶ Declaring a property
- ▶ Compounding properties

Introduction

In this chapter, we will be reviewing events. Normally, someone experienced in programming languages understands the concept behind the behavior of an event. The most common definition of an event is something that happens, and usually GUI frameworks provide a way to handle things that happen. Kivy is not the exception, even thought Kivy does it in an easier way than the others.

The following recipes will cover three types of events: clock-related, widget-defined, and property events. **Clock-related events are** events where time plays a relevant role. The **widget-defined** events are those that are related to the widget's functionality. For example, in the case of a button, when it is pressed, an event is fired. A **property event** is fired when a property of the widget is changed, such as size or position.

Scheduling a one-time event

A **one-time event** is one of those clock-related events where you perform an event just once after some time has passed.

Getting ready

In this recipe, it is assumed that the reader is acquainted with the Kv language and widgets, especially with labels. Also, we will implement the concept of using a mouse to perform the actions that we learned in *Chapter 2, Input, Motion, and Touch*, particularly for this recipe, *using the mouse* to perform the actions.

How to do it...

To complete this recipe, follow these steps:

1. First, in the KV file, let's declare an empty label. You can do this by using the following code:

    ```
    <MyW>:
        Label:
            id: label1
            pos: 200,200
            text: ''
    ```

2. Then in the Python code, import the Clock object instance.

3. In the widget class, define the method my_callback(), which will be fired.

4. Also, override the on_touch_down() method where we will schedule the event, using the following code:

    ```
    import kivy

    from kivy.app import App
    from kivy.uix.widget import Widget
    from kivy.clock import Clock

    class MyW(Widget):

        def my_callback(self, dt):
            self.ids.label1.text = 'My callback is called
            ! ' + str(dt)
    ```

```
    def on_touch_down(self, touch):
        Clock.schedule_once(self.my_callback, 1)

class e1App(App):

    def build(self):
        return MyW()

if __name__ == '__main__':
    e1App().run()
```

How it works...

The KV file is the usual definition for a label where the initial text is empty. Remember that the rule name must be the name of the root widget class in the Python code.

Now, in the Python code, the first three lines are the same as those that we use to work with Kivy and its widgets. The fourth line is:

```
from kivy.clock import Clock
```

This line is necessary to schedule the event; it is the class to use the `Clock` object. The fifth line is:

```
class MyW(Widget):
```

This is the line where the class for the rule starts. Its name must be the same as the Kivy rule in the KV file. Next is the sixth line of the code:

```
    def my_callback(self, dt):
```

This is where we define the function that will be fired when the event happens. The seventh line is:

```
self.ids.label1.text = 'My callback is called
! ' + str(dt)
```

We have replaced the text of our empty label defined in the KV file with text and `dt`, which is the time interval. We are using the `str()` method because only strings can be seen in the label. The eighth line is:

```
def on_touch_down(self, touch):
```

This is where we define the actions performed when the touch occurs inside of our app. The ninth line is:

```
    Clock.schedule_once(self.my_callback, 1)
```

This line is where the magic happens; here we schedule a one-time event, and this event is to call the function method `my_callback`. It will occur after a second has passed, and then `Clock.schedule_once()` is called. See how this is defined in the second parameter of the method `Clock.schedule_once()`. The rest of the lines are common and will help us execute our app using Kivy.

There's more...

We have a few more things to share about the `Clock.schedule_once()` method. As we have pointed out, the second parameter is where we define the time interval. However, sometimes, we need to perform the event as soon as possible; we can do this by providing *0* as the second parameter, and usually it fires immediately after the next frame. It is also possible to fire the event before the next frame or set different one-time events. This is possible if we use a *-1* instance instead of the *0* as the second parameter. All events scheduled with the *-1* will be fired before the next frame.

See also

To know more about the app frames, refer the recipes in *Chapter 5*, *Graphics – Canvas and Instructions*.

Scheduling a repetitive event

After our first recipe, we can think about how to schedule a repetitive event. The present recipe will use one touch in the app to schedule the event and a double touch to unschedule the event.

Getting ready

We will use the knowledge about inputs from *Chapter 2*, *Input, Motion, and Touch*, particularly for this recipe, and will use multitouching to perform our actions. Also, it is useful to know that the label is a basic widget in the Kv language.

How to do it...

To complete this recipe, perform the following listed steps:

1. First, in the KV file, declare an empty label. The following code will help you do this:

```
<MyW>:
    Label:
        id: label1
        pos: 200,200
        text: ''
```

2. In the Python code, import the `Clock` object instance.

3. In the `widget` class, define the method `my_callback()`, which is the method that will be fired.

4. Also, override the method `on_touch_down()` where we can schedule the repetitive event.

5. With an `if` statement, select a double tap and unschedule the event:

```
import kivy

from kivy.app import App
from kivy.uix.widget import Widget
from kivy.clock import Clock

class MyW(Widget):

    def my_callback(self, dt):
        self.ids.label1.text = 'My callback is called ' +
        str(dt)

    def on_touch_down(self, touch):
        Clock.schedule_interval(self.my_callback, 1 / 30.)
        if touch.is_double_tap:
            self.ids.label1.text = ''
            Clock.unschedule(self.my_callback)

class e2App(App):

    def build(self):
        return MyW()

if __name__ == '__main__':
    e2App().run()
```

How it works...

Here again in the KV file, there is a usual definition for a label where the initial text is empty. However, let's remember that the rule name will be the name for the widget class in the Python code.

Now, in the Python code, the first three lines form the code that permit us to work with Kivy and its widgets. The fourth line is:

```
from kivy.clock import Clock
```

This line is necessary to schedule the event; it is the instance of the `Clock` object. The fifth line is:

```
class MyW(Widget):
```

This is where the class for the rule starts; its name must be the same as the Kivy rule in the KV file. The following is the sixth line of the code:

```
def my_callback(self, dt):
```

This is where we define the callback method that will be fired when the event takes places. The seventh line is:

```
self.ids.label1.text = 'My callback is called
! ' + str(dt)
```

We have replaced the text of our empty label defined in the KV file with text and `dt`, which is the time interval. We make sure that `dt` is a string that uses the `str()` method because only strings can be seen in the label. The eighth line is:

```
def on_touch_down(self, touch):
```

This is where we define the actions performed when the touch occurs inside of our app. The ninth line is:

```
Clock.schedule_interval(self.my_callback, 1/30.)
```

In this line, we schedule the repetitive event where the callback function `my_callback` is called and the event will be performed 30 times per second. The tenth line is:

```
if touch.is_double_tap:
```

This is where we select the double taps made in our app. The eleventh line is:

```
self.ids.label1.text = ''
```

Here, we clean the label so that it can be empty again. The twelfth line is:

```
Clock.unschedule(self.my_callback)
```

This is the statement that will unschedule the repetitive event. The rest of the lines are common and will help us execute our app using Kivy.

There's more...

There is another way to unschedule the event; basically, if the `my_callback()` method returns the output as **false**, then the event will be automatically unscheduled. We need to add a new variable count to the widget class, and modify the `my_callback()` method by adding codes, something like this:

```
global count
count += 1
if count == 10:
print 'Last call of my callback, bye bye !'
return False
```

Now, if the method is called 10 times, the event will be unscheduled.

See also

To learn more about widgets, see the recipes in *Chapter 4, Widgets*.

Triggering events

If we want to schedule the events, we can trigger them, which will help you trigger the same event in different parts of your code. In the next described recipe, the event will be triggered when we double tap.

Getting ready

Again, we are going to make use of the double tap, so it is important that you refer to the recipes in *Chapter 2, Input, Motion, and Touch*. Even though the skeleton of the code is similar to that for the last event, the actions are completely different. Here the unscheduling will be automatic.

How to do it...

Perform the following steps to achieve the goal:

1. First, in the KV file, declare an empty label using the following code:

```
<MyW>:
    Label:
        id: label1
        pos: 200,200
        text: ''
```

2. In the Python code, import the `Clock` object instance.

3. In the widget class, define the method `my_callback()`.

4. Also, define the method `on_touch_down()` where we will define the trigger.

5. As shown in the following code, using an `if` statement, select a double tap and fire the event.

```python
import kivy

from kivy.app import App
from kivy.uix.widget import Widget
from kivy.clock import Clock

class MyW(Widget):

    def my_callback(self,dt):
        self.ids.label1.text = 'My callback is called ! ' +
        str(dt)

    def on_touch_down(self, touch):
        trigger = Clock.create_trigger(self.my_callback)
        if touch.is_double_tap:
            trigger()

class e3App(App):

    def build(self):
        return MyW()

if __name__ == '__main__':
    e3App().run()
```

How it works...

The declared KV file is the usual definition for a label where the initial text is empty, but let's remember that the rule name will be the name for the widget class in the Python code.

Let's now review the Python code; the first three lines permit us to work with Kivy and its widgets. The fourth line is:

```python
from kivy.clock import Clock
```

This line is necessary to trigger the event. The fifth line is:

```python
class MyW(Widget):
```

This is the line where the class for the rule starts; its name must be the same as the Kivy rule in the KV file. Next is the sixth line:

```
def my_callback(self, dt):
```

This is where we define the function that will be fired when the event happens. The seventh line is:

```
self.ids.label1.text = 'My callback is called
! ' + str(dt)
```

We have replaced the text of our empty label defined in the KV file with text and `dt`, which is the time interval. We are using the `str()` method because only strings can be seen in the label. The eighth line is:

```
def on_touch_down(self, touch):
```

This is where we define the actions that will be performed when the touch occurs inside of our app. The ninth line is :

```
trigger = Clock.create_trigger(self.my_callback)
```

In this line, we create the trigger that will fire the function callback `my_callback`, and it will perform a callback. The next line is the tenth line:

```
if touch.is_double_tap:
```

This is where we select the double taps made in our app. The eleventh is:

```
trigger()
```

Here, we have fired our defined trigger, which will be unscheduled automatically. The rest of the lines are quite common and will help us execute our app using Kivy.

There's more...

The `Clock.create_trigger()` method also admits a second parameter, which has the same functionality as the function method `Clock.schedule_once()`. We can define a timeout to delay the firing of the event.

See also

To learn more about widgets, see the recipes in *Chapter 4, Widgets*.

Defining widget events

Now, we will study the events that are called widget-defined events. These kinds of events are inherent to the widget. This recipe will illustrate it with probably the most common widget—the button. We will perform two events: one when the button is pressed and the other when the button state is changed.

Getting ready

In this recipe, it is necessary to clear the difference between the state of the button and press action. Because the states of the button are not pressed and no pressed, they actually are normal and down. The press action changes between both states of the button.

How to do it...

To accomplish the end goal, follow these steps:

1. First in the KV file, declare an empty label using the following code:

```
<MyW>:
    Label:
        id: label1
        pos: 200,200
        text: ''
```

2. In the Python code, define the widget class.

3. In the widget class, define constructor __init__() within a button.

4. Bind the callback methods to the button.

5. Define the state_callback and on_press_callback methods with the actions to be performed:

```
import kivy

from kivy.app import App
from kivy.uix.widget import Widget
from kivy.uix.button import Button

class MyW(Widget):

    def __init__(self, **kwargs):
        super(MyW, self).__init__(**kwargs)
        btn = Button(text='click me')
        btn.bind(on_press=self.on_press_callback,
        state=self.state_callback)
```

```
            self.add_widget(btn)

    def state_callback(self, obj, value):
        print obj, value

    def on_press_callback(self, obj):
        self.ids.label1.text = 'press on button'

class e4App(App):

    def build(self):
        return MyW()

if __name__ == '__main__':
    e4App().run()
```

How it works...

The KV file is the usual definition for a label where the initial text is empty. Remember that the rule name must be the name of the widget class in the Python code.

Let's review the Python code; the first three lines will permit us to work with Kivy and its widgets. The fourth line is:

```
from kivy.uix.button import Button
```

This line is necessary to use the button, and it imports the button widget. The fifth line is:

```
class MyW(Widget):
```

This is the line where the class for the rule starts; its name must be the same as the Kivy rule in the KV file. Next, the sixth line is:

```
def __init__(self, **kwargs):
```

This is the initial method that always helps execute the code. The seventh line is a usual Python sentence to relate the self object to the MyW class. The eighth line creates the button and its characteristics. The next line is:

```
btn.bind(on_press=self.on_press_callback,
    state=self.state_callback)
```

This line is where we do the binding with the callback methods, which we will define later in the code. In the tenth line, we add the button to the app. The eleventh and twelfth lines of code are as follows:

```
def state_callback(self, obj, value):
    print obj, value
```

These lines are the method called when the state of the button is changed. At that moment, in the console, the function will print the `obj` address and the value of its state property. The thirteenth and fourteenth lines are:

```
def on_press_callback(self, obj):
    self.ids.label1.text = 'press on button'
```

Here we define the action performed when the button is pressed and change the the empty label. The rest of the lines are common code that will help us execute our app using Kivy.

There's more...

There is something to explore, as our class, MyW, is a Kivy object itself and we can bind an action to its widget-defined event; something like this:

```
self.bind(pos=self.on_press_callback)
```

If the position of the main Kivy object changes, the `on_press_callback` method will be fired.

See also

To learn more about widgets, see the recipes in *Chapter 4, Widgets*.

Creating custom events

Another possibility with events is that we can create and customize our own events. There are many situations where we could need a custom event; for example, when we create our own widget. This recipe will create a new event that will fire an action when the label of the button is changed.

Getting ready

Now we need a more complex recipe, and it is useful for the reader to review the recipes first before getting into the content of custom events in Kivy. We will also use the Kv language to design the widgets, so we assume that the reader is familiar with the Kv language or has gone through the first chapter.

How to do it...

Use the following steps to achieve the end goal:

1. First, in the KV file, declare an empty label and a button using the following code:

```
<MyW>:
    Button:
        id: button1
        text: 'Hello'
    Label:
        id: label1
        pos: 200,200
        text: ''
```

2. In the Python code, define the widget class.

3. In the widget class, define the __init__() constructor within a registered event type.

4. Also, in the widget class, define the method on_swipe() with the event process.

5. Define the method do_something, which dispatches the event.

6. Define the on_touch_down method to perform the change of the label:

```
import kivy

from kivy.app import App
from kivy.uix.widget import Widget

class MyW(Widget):
    def __init__(self, **kwargs):
        super(MyW, self).__init__(**kwargs)
        self.register_event_type('on_swipe')

    def on_swipe(self, value):
        if self.ids.button1.text != 'Hello':
            self.ids.label1.text = 'Hello1'

    def do_something(self, value):
        self.dispatch('on_swipe', value)
```

```
        def on_touch_down(self, touch):
            self.ids.button1.text = 'xxx'
            self.do_something('test')

    class e5App(App):
        def build(self):
            return MyW()

    if __name__ == '__main__':
        e5App().run()
```

How it works...

Let's start with the KV file where we will define the empty label and the button. Note that we are providing the initial text for the button that we need in our event.

In the Python code, we have three initial lines, which are used for Kivy and widgets. The fourth code line is the definition of the widget class. Next is the fifth line:

```
    def __init__(self, **kwargs):
```

This is the initial method that always executes, the constructor. The sixth line is a usual Python sentence that relates the `self` object to the `MyW` class. The seventh line is:

```
        self.register_event_type('on_swipe')
```

This is the line where the custom event is registered; we use the name `on_swipe` for the event. We must have the method `on_swipe()`, where the specific event instructions are declared. Here, we have to say that the name on the event type must start with the prefix `on`, such as `on_swipe()`. The following ninth and tenth lines are the definition of the method `on_swipe()`:

```
        if self.ids.button1.text != 'Hello':
            self.ids.label1.text = 'Hello1'
```

These are where we compare the label of the button with the original label, and if they do not match, the event will change the empty label of the text to `Hello1`. The eleventh and twelfth lines are listed here:

```
    def do_something(self, value):
        self.dispatch('on_swipe', value)
```

Here, we are creating a method that dispatches the event `on_swipe` and if we want to test the event, we just have to call this method. The thirteenth line is where we detect the touch in our app and execute the subsequent lines. The fourteenth line of code is here:

```
        self.ids.button1.text = 'xxx'
```

We will modify the content of the text in the button. The fifteenth line is:

```
self.do_something('test')
```

This line will call the method that fires the event, and finally the test is performed. The rest of the code is necessary and will help us execute our app.

There's more...

Something that needs to be highlighted is how we are making the test. If the button's text has changed in the same method as the event, which works well for our recipe, but for every technical aspect, the event actually occurs even thought the button has not been modified. So, if we actually want to prevent the event when nothing has been changed, it is in the `do_something()` method where the check must be done. Thus, our `do_something()` method must look like this:

```
def do_something(self, value):
    if self.ids.button1.text != 'Hello':
        self.dispatch('on_swipe', value)
```

See also

To learn more about widgets, see the recipes in *Chapter 4*, *Widgets*.

Attaching callbacks

Now, we have created a new kind of event, so it is possible to attach callback methods to our new event as we have in the predefined events. For this recipe, we will create a new event and attach a callback function to it. If the button text changes, the event as in the past recipe will be fired.

Getting ready

We will use the code from the previous recipe as the base of this recipe and will add a different touch so that we can change the button when it is double tapped. Hence, I would advise you to go through the previous recipe again. Also, the reader may find the section on multitouching from *Chapter 2*, *Input, Motion, and Touch* useful specifically.

How to do it...

Perform the following steps:

1. First, in the KV file, declare an empty label and a button:

```
<MyW>:
    Button:
        id: button1
        text: 'Hello'
    Label:
        id: label1
        pos: 200,200
        text: ''
```

2. In the Python code, define the callback method.

3. Define the widget class.

4. In the widget class, define the constructor method `__init__()` within a register event type and the method `on_swipe()` with the event process.

5. Define the method `do_something` that dispatches the event.

6. Define the `on_touch_down` method to perform the change of the button.

7. Use a triple tap to return the button to its original state.

8. Use the following code:

```
import kivy

from kivy.app import App
from kivy.uix.widget import Widget

def my_callback(value, *args):
    print "Hello, I got an event!", args

class MyW(Widget):
    def __init__(self, **kwargs):
        super(MyW, self).__init__(**kwargs)
        self.register_event_type('on_swipe')

    def on_swipe(self, value):
        self.ids.label1.text = 'Hello1'

    def do_something(self, value):
        if self.ids.button1.text != 'Hello':
            self.dispatch('on_swipe', value)
```

```
def on_touch_down(self, touch):
    if touch.is_double_tap:
        self.ids.button1.text = 'xxx'
    if touch.is_triple_tap:
        self.ids.button1.text = 'Hello'
    self.bind(on_swipe=my_callback)
    self.do_something('test')

class e6App(App):

    def build(self):
        return MyW()

if __name__ == '__main__':
    e6App().run()
```

How it works...

The KV file has the declaration of the label and the widget. Note that the initial text of the button is provided here.

Now, in the Python code, after the usual first three lines, we have the following method:

```
def my_callback(value, *args):
    print "Hello, I got an event!", args
```

This method is out of the widget class and can be used as a callback function that will print **Hello, I got an event!**, args on the console. The next line is our old knowledge declaration of the widget class. The __init__ function remains similar as in the previous recipe with the sentence that registers the kind of event. The next method is:

```
def on_swipe(self, value):
    self.ids.label1.text = 'Hello1'
```

This is the action performed when the event is fired. In this case, it will change the empty label of the text to Hello1. The next method is:

```
def do_something(self, value):
    if self.ids.button1.text != 'Hello':
        self.dispatch('on_swipe', value)
```

Here, we perform the actions that dispatch the event with the test, which verifies whether the event has to be dispatched or not. The last method inside the widget class is as follows:

```
def on_touch_down(self, touch):
    if touch.is_double_tap:
        self.ids.button1.text = 'xxx'
    if touch.is_triple_tap:
        self.ids.button1.text = 'Hello'
    self.bind(on_swipe=my_callback)
    self.do_something('test')
```

This is where we change the button text by taking advantage of the touch action in our app. If the user does a double tap, we change the text from the original, and if the tap is triple, we change the text to the original. In this method, we also use the `self.bind()` function that attaches the callback function to the `on_swipe` event. The last line calls the `do_something` method, which tests if the event has been dispatched. The rest of the file contains necessary code, which will help us execute our app.

See also

To learn more about widgets, see the recipes in *Chapter 4, Widgets*.

Declaring a property

This recipe will work with the last type of events, which is the property event. To be very specific, we will create an invisible widget that will fire an event when a selected property is changed. Just to identify of this invisible widget, we surround it with two normal buttons; thus, the section between them is our invisible widget.

Getting ready

The properties in Kivy have been reviewed in *Chapter 1, Kivy and the Kv language*, specifically with in the *Declaring properties within a class* recipe. Thus, it will be useful to refer to this recipe and also to the section on multitouching from *Chapter 2, Input, Motion, and Touch*.

How to do it...

The recipe is:

1. First, import the `ListProperty` from Kivy properties.
2. Create the class for the root widget.
3. Add two button widgets into the root widget.
4. Reference the `CustomBtn` widget, bind it, and add it.

5. Create the class for the `CustomBtn` widget and declare the `ListProperty`.
6. Define the `on_touch_down` method to perform the change of the property.
7. Define the `on_pressed` method, which performs the action when the event is fired.

```
import kivy

from kivy.app import App
from kivy.uix.widget import Widget
from kivy.uix.button import Button
from kivy.properties import ListProperty

class RootWidget(Widget):

    def __init__(self, **kwargs):
        super(RootWidget, self).__init__(**kwargs)
        self.add_widget(Button(text='btn 1',
        pos=(0,100)))
        self.add_widget(Button(text='btn 2',
        pos=(100,0)))
        cb = CustomBtn()
        cb.bind(pressed=self.btn_pressed)
        self.add_widget(cb)

    def btn_pressed(self, instance, pos):
        print ('pos: printed from root widget:
        {pos}'.format(pos=pos))

class CustomBtn(Widget):

    pressed = ListProperty([0, 0])

    def on_touch_down(self, touch):
        if self.collide_point(*touch.pos):
            self.pressed = touch.pos
            return True
        return super(CustomBtn,
        self).on_touch_down(touch)

    def on_pressed(self, instance, pos):
        print ('pressed at {pos}'.format(pos=pos))

class e7App(App):
    def build(self):
        return RootWidget()
if __name__ == '__main__':
    e7App().run()
```

How it works...

The first four lines of the code are common and help us use Kivy, the widgets, and the buttons. In the fifth line, we import the property that we will use as a trigger of the event, in this case, `ListProperty`. In the sixth line, we define the class for the `RootWidget`, and the seventh line defines the `__init__()` method. The following is the eighth line:

```
super(RootWidget, self).__init__(**kwargs)
```

This is used to call the constructor of the parent class (in this case, `Widget`) when it's overridden, as it does important event-managing stuff that can't be skipped. The ninth and tenth lines are where we add two buttons to the `RootWidget` class; note that we provide position information to them because we cannot use the default position for both. The eleventh line is as follows:

```
cb = CustomBtn()
```

Here, we are associating the custom button class that is defined later in the code with this variable `cb`. Next, the twelfth line is:

```
cb.bind(pressed=self.btn_pressed)
```

This is where we bind the fired event with the `btn_pressed` callback method declared in the same class. Then, if the event is fired, this method will be executed. The thirteenth line is where we add the custom button, which is a widget itself, to the `RootWidget`. The fourteenth and fifteenth lines are where we have the method that is executed when the event occurs. In this case, we print on the console the position of the touch that fires the event. The sixteenth line is:

```
class CustomBtn(Widget):
```

This line defines the class for the custom button. Note that it is also a widget. The seventeenth line is:

```
pressed = ListProperty([0, 0])
```

This is where the magic begins. Here we relate the pressed variable with a property, in this case, `ListProperty`, which has a [0,0] default value, and now any change made to this value will produce an event. Next, the eighteenth line defines of the `on_touch_down` method, which helps to detect the touch. The nineteenth line is:

```
if self.collide_point(*touch.pos):
```

This is a conditional sentence that permits the selection those touches that occur in the area of the custom widget. The twentieth line is:

```
self.pressed = touch.pos
```

This line will fire the event if the touch does not occur in the position that is stored in the `pressed` variable, which was [0,0] at the beginning. The next two lines are not relevant for this recipe; the result will be the same without those lines, but they are necessary if we have more widgets that needs information on touch. Finally, the method is as follows:

```
def on_pressed(self, instance, pos):
    print ('pressed at {pos}'.format(pos=pos))
```

This method needs to have the name `on_pressed` because Kivy is familiar only with this name and will execute this method when the pressed property is changed. Hence, there must be a method with the prefix `on` for our property event. The rest of the code is standard and will help you run our app with Kivy.

There's more...

Every property in a widget will fire an event, so we can work with all properties of Kivy, even custom-defined properties. For example, in this recipe, we can use the `StringProperty` instance, instead of `ListProperty`; let's import the `StringProperty` and change the seventeenth line to:

```
pressed = StringProperty([0, 0])
```

The twentieth line becomes:

```
self.pressed = str(touch.pos)
```

This last change is because the `StringProperty` just receives strings. With these three little changes, we have the same result in our app using a different property.

See also

This recipe will relate to *Chapter 6, Advanced Graphics – Shaders and Rendering*, specifically to the recipe *Creating Widgets*. So check it out.

Compounding properties

While working with properties in Kivy, there are times when we will have to create our own property that usually is a compound of some standard properties.

Getting ready

Again, for this recipe, it is important to understand the properties in Kivy that have been reviewed in *Chapter 1, Kivy and the Kv language*, articular in the *Declaring properties within a class* recipe. We will be learning in detail about `AliasProperty`, in which you need to create a custom getter and setter methods that fit your needs.

How to do it...

For this recipe, follow these steps:

1. Define a getter method in your code.
2. Define the setter method.
3. Create the reference for `AliasProperty`.
4. Define the method to fire the event:

```
def get_right(self):
    return self.x + self.width

def set_right(self, value):
    self.x = value - self.width

right = AliasProperty(get_right, set_right,
bind=('x', 'width'))
    def on_right():
        print "Hello"
```

How it works...

The first line defines the getter method, which will get the information for the property that we are creating. In the second line, we have the return method that adds the position in x and the `width`. The third line defines the setter method, which is the modification that the property will do; in this case, the position in x will be changed by the subtraction of the `width` from the `value`. The fifth line is:

```
right = AliasProperty(get_right, set_right,
bind=('x', 'width'))
```

Here, it assigns of the custom property; let's note that the third parameter of `AliasProperty`, the `bind`, is the method defined when the event is dispatched. In this case, the event is dispatched when any argument of the `bind()` method changes that is the position in x or the width of our widget. The last method is:

```
def on_right():
    print "Hello"
```

Again, as for all the property events, we could execute these instructions when the event is fired. In this case, it would print **Hello** on the console.

There's more...

An interesting fact is that we can create read-only properties in this way, by just taking the setter and defining it as None; in this case, the property will not set anything in the app. Our fifth line looks like this:

```
right = AliasProperty(get_right,None,bind=('x', 'width'))
```

See also

Again this recipe is related to the recipe *Creating Widgets* in *Chapter 6, Advanced Graphics – Shaders and Rendering*.

4
Widgets

In this chapter, we will cover:

- ▸ Using the basics: buttons, labels, and text inputs
- ▸ Manipulating the widget tree
- ▸ Traversing the tree
- ▸ Using swappable widgets
- ▸ Organizing with layouts
- ▸ Using FloatLayout
- ▸ Using BoxLayout
- ▸ Using GridLayout
- ▸ Using StackLayout
- ▸ Using RelativeLayout
- ▸ Using AnchorLayout
- ▸ Working with ActionBar

Introduction

Widgets have become common in GUI frameworks, and nowadays even a user can easily interact with and configure them. For our purpose, we define the widgets as elements of interaction that are reusable. They are those graphical elements, which are important pieces of the human-machine interface.

For a Kivy framework, the widgets play an important role, not just because Kivy is a graphical framework, but also because it intends to organize the GUI as a tree of widgets with a root widget in which the other widgets live. Kivy itself has a bunch of predefined widgets that you can use in your app or as part of your own widget. The special kinds that we will be describing in this chapter are layouts, which help us in a visual organization of our tree of widgets.

Using the basics: buttons, labels, and text inputs

Here, we will work with basic widgets as the first approach to the chapter topic. In our task, we will develop an app that has three elements: a text input, a button, and a label. Using this, the user can modify the label by pressing the button, by moving the cursor into the text input, or by changing the text input.

Getting ready

In the following few recipes, we are going to intensively use Kv language, so it is important for you to read *Chapter 1, Kivy and the Kv language* or at least the recipe *Accessing widgets defined inside Kv language in your Python code* from the first chapter.

How to do it...

To complete the task, follow these steps:

1. In the KV file, define a label.
2. Also define the button with an `on_press reference` method to a callback method.
3. The text input with `on_focus reference` to another callback method is:

```
<MyW>:
    Label:
        id: label1
        pos: 300,200
        text: 'Hello'
    Button:
        id: button1
        pos: 200,300
        size: 300,50
        text: 'Hello'
        on_press: root.my_callback()
    TextInput:
        id: textinput1
        pos: 200,400
        size: 300,50
        multiline: False
        text: 'ddd'
        on_focus: root.my_callback1(self.text)
```

4. In the Python file, define the callback method that changes the label, indicating that the button has been pressed.

5. Define another callback method that changes the label with the text inserted in the text input widget.

```
import kivy
kivy.require('1.9.0') # replace with your current kivy
version !

from kivy.app import App
from kivy.uix.widget import Widget

class MyW(Widget):

    def my_callback(self):
        self.ids.label1.text = 'Click ! '

    def my_callback1(self, inpt):
        self.ids.label1.text = 'Enter ! ' + str(inpt)

class e1App(App):

    def build(self):
        return MyW()

if __name__ == '__main__':
    e1App().run()
```

How it works...

The KV file has the definition of the three widgets that we use in this app. The first widget is the label that we already used in the preceding chapters. Something to emphasize is how important it is to specify the position of the widgets to avoid overlap with the other widgets. The second widget is the button where we specify the size of the widget and the `on_press` action that links the Python code. The last widget—the text input—has more options than the previous widgets; here we are linking the second callback method in the class of the root with the event that is fired when the text input is in focus.

In the Python file, we have a class of root widget with the two callback methods that we already used in the previous chapters.

There's more...

Always, it is possible to dispense the KV file and directly add the widgets in the Python code using the `add_widget()` method in the `__init__()` method of the root widget class. For example, in our Python code in the `MyW()` class, let's add the following:

```
def __init__(self, **kwargs):
    super(MyW, self).__init__(**kwargs)
    self.add_widget(Button(text='button2', pos=(100,100)))
```

Also, you have to import the button widget:

```
from kivy.uix.button import Button
```

This is not necessary if you add the button directly in the KV file.

See also

You can explore more about the predefined Kivy widgets at `http://kivy.org/docs/gettingstarted/examples.html` in the **Widgets** section.

Manipulating the widget tree

Now, we want to give more flexibility to our apps. There are situations when we have to add or remove widgets at the execution time, which results in a direct manipulation of the app's widget tree. In this recipe, we will develop an app that will add buttons with a click and will remove all widgets with a triple-click. We will use the double-click to remove a specific widget.

Getting ready

We will use the widget tree in this recipe, so it could be useful to review the recipe *Referencing widgets* in *Chapter 1, Kivy and the Kv language*. Also, we will be working with multitapping, so you either need to have your basics clear or refer to *Detecting multitapping* recipe from *Chapter 2, Input, Motion, and Touch*.

How to do it...

We will use two files: the KV file with the widgets and a Python file with the instructions to manipulate the widget tree. Follow the next steps:

1. In the KV file, define a label using the following code:

```
<MyW>:
    Label:
```

```
        id: label1
        pos: 300,200
        text: 'Hello'
```

2. In the Python file, create the `on_touch_down()` method.

3. Inside the same method, when a double tap is detected, use `remove_widget()` to remove the label.

4. Also when a triple tap is detected, use the `clear_widgets()` method to clear all the widgets in the app as follows:

```python
import kivy
from kivy.app import App
from kivy.uix.widget import Widget
from kivy.uix.button import Button

class MyW(Widget):

    def on_touch_down(self, touch):
        self.add_widget(Button(text=str(touch.pos),
        pos=touch.pos))
        if touch.is_double_tap:
            self.remove_widget(self.ids.label1)
        if touch.is_triple_tap:
            self.clear_widgets()

class e2App(App):

    def build(self):
        return MyW()

if __name__ == '__main__':
    e2App().run()
```

How it works...

In the Python file, the initial lines are the same as we use with Kivy. The fourth line has the import of the button widget, necessary to use and reference this kind of widgets in the Python code. The seventh line is:

```python
self.add_widget(Button(text=str(touch.pos),pos=touch.pos))
```

This is where we add the button to the root widget. Note how the setting options are used as the parameters of the method here. The ninth line is:

```python
self.remove_widget(self.ids.label1)
```

This line removes a specific widget, the one with the `label1` ID. The eleventh line is as follows:

```
self.clear_widgets()
```

Here we are cleaning the widget tree. Specifically, we are removing all the children of the root widget, which is defined by the class in which we are using the `clear_widgets()` method. Such subtlety is important for bigger widget trees.

There's more...

The order of drawing widgets is based on its position in the widget tree. The last widget's canvas is drawn last, on top of everything else inside its parent. The `add_widget` method takes an index parameter to change this, and it lets you handle the drawing order:

```
add_widget(widget, index)
```

In Kivy, this index is called **z-index**.

See also

In this section, you can list other recipes that are related to this task; we can update the specific titles later if they haven't been written yet.

This section is optional—if there are no other recipes related to the task, then just delete it.

Traversing the tree

There are situations when you need to go through the app's widget tree. This recipe will use a tap to add new buttons to the root widgets and double tap to print the children of the root widget in the console. Again, triple tap will clean the widgets of our app.

Getting ready

The code for this recipe is similar to the previous recipe, so you can refer to them and apply the same to this recipe.

How to do it...

For this recipe, follow the next steps:

1. In the KV file, define a label using the following code:

    ```
    <MyW>:
        Label:
            id: label1
            pos: 200,200
            text: 'Hello'
    ```

2. In the Python file, create the on_touch_down() method to add a button every time that a touch is performed.

3. Inside the same method, when double tap is detected, traverse the children property with self.children and print the child in the console.

4. Also when a triple tap is detected, use the clear_widgets() method as shown in the following code to clear all the widgets in the app:

    ```
    import kivy

    from kivy.app import App
    from kivy.uix.widget import Widget
    from kivy.uix.button import Button

    class MyW(Widget):

        def on_touch_down(self, touch):
            self.add_widget(Button(text=str(touch.pos),
            pos=touch.pos))
            if touch.is_double_tap:
                for child in self.children:
                    print(child)
            if touch.is_triple_tap:
                self.clear_widgets()

    class e3App(App):

        def build(self):
            return MyW()

    if __name__ == '__main__':
        e3App().run()
    ```

How it works...

The Python code is similar to the code in the previous recipe, so let's focus on the review of the ninth line:

```
for child in self.children:
```

This is for the loop that will be traversing the children list in order and assigning the current child to the `child` variable. The children property is `ListProperty`. We print this variable to the console in the tenth line of the code.

Using swappable widgets

There are some situations wherein you need to shift a widget, but then you realize that it is not necessary to define a new class for it. This is what we call the **dynamics class**, which allows us to work with different widgets. In this recipe, we want to create some buttons from a list that will swap a label in the app. Here, we will be using the screen manager widget.

Getting ready

This recipe is based on some advanced KV concepts, thus it is advisable to read the recipe *Reusing styles in multiple widgets* from *Chapter 1, Kivy and the Kv language*. Also go through the previous recipe *Manipulating the widgets tree* to understand the differences between them.

How to do it...

To complete this task, follow the next steps:

1. In the KV file, define `BoxLayout` to accommodate the buttons.
2. Define a screen manager widget.
3. In the `Mbutton` rule, define the `on_press` action that will change the current widget in the screen manager as follows:

```
<MyW>:
    orientation: 'vertical'
    BoxLayout:
        size_hint_y: None
        height: 30
        id: buttons
    ScreenManager:
        id: sm


<MButton>:
    on_press: app.root.ids.sm.current = self.text
```

4. In the Python code, build a list with the six elements.

5. Declare a class for the rule `<MButton>`.

6. In the class for the `<MyW>` rule, traverse the list with a `for` loop and add the labels in the screen manager widget and the buttons in the `BoxLayout` as follows:

```python
from kivy.app import App
from kivy.lang import Builder
from kivy.uix.label import Label
from kivy.uix.button import Button
from kivy.uix.boxlayout import BoxLayout
from kivy.uix.screenmanager import Screen

letters = ["txt 1","txt 2","txt 3","txt 5", "txt 6"]

class MButton(Button):
    pass

class MyW(BoxLayout):
    def __init__(self, **kwargs):
        super(MyW, self).__init__(**kwargs)
        for l in letters:
            s = Screen(name=l)
            s.add_widget(Label(text=l))
            self.ids.sm.add_widget(s)
            self.ids.buttons.add_widget(MButton(text=l))

class e4App(App):

    def build(self):
        return MyW()

if __name__ == '__main__':
    e4App().run()
```

How it works...

Here the magic is done by the `MButton()` class that serves as a link with the `<MButton>` rule in the KV file, which works when all the buttons added.

If you want to know more about the screen manager widget, you should look at `http://kivy.org/docs/api-kivy.uix.screenmanager.html`

Organizing with layouts

Sometimes, it is quite tedious to establish each and every position for all the widgets in our app. There is a special kind of widget, the layouts widget, that makes things easy for us. In this recipe, we will review how to work with the size and position hints that allows us to organize widgets inside this new kind of widget.

Getting ready

A quick check of the recipe *Designing with the Kv language* in *Chapter 1, Kivy and the Kv language* could be important to go deeper in this recipe.

How to do it...

To complete the task, perform the following steps:

1. In the KV file, define two buttons and assign the `size_hint` and `pos_hint` properties as follows:

   ```
   <MyW1>:
       Button:
           id: label1
           size_hint: .2, .2
           pos_hint: {'center_x':.5, 'center_y': .5}
           text: 'B1'
       Button:
           id: label2
           size_hint: .1, .1
           pos_hint: {'center_x':.1, 'center_y': .1}
           text: 'B2'
   ```

2. In the Python file, import the `FloatLayout`.

3. Define the class for the rule in the KV file.

4. In the `__init__` constructor, give a size to the `FloatLayout` method.

5. Define the root class that will define the root widget.

6. In the `__init__` constructor, add the `FloatLayout` method to the root widget as follows:

```
import kivy
kivy.require('1.9.0') # replace with your current kivy version !

from kivy.app import App
from kivy.uix.widget import Widget
from kivy.uix.floatlayout import FloatLayout

class MyW(Widget):
    def __init__(self, **kwargs):
        super(MyW, self).__init__(**kwargs)
        self.MyW1_name=MyW1()
        self.add_widget(self.MyW1_name)

class MyW1(FloatLayout):
    def __init__(self, **kwargs):
        super(MyW1, self).__init__(**kwargs)
        self.size=(300,300)

class e5App(App):

    def build(self):
        return MyW()

if __name__ == '__main__':
    e5App().run()
```

How it works...

The layout widgets allow us to organize the widgets in our app, but they are not completely smart, so you will need to provide some information to them. This is reflected in the KV file of this recipe; we need to introduce the `size_hint` and `pos_hint` properties for the button widgets. In case of the `size_hint` property, we set the size of the button, which will be a percentage of the layout size. For the first button, it is 20 percent in height and width, and for the second button, it is 10 percent. The `pos_hint` property provides a notion for localization of the widget in the layout with this percentage relative to the size of the widget. It is useful because the `pos` setting is relative to the size of the whole app. The `center_x` or `center_y` instructions help us localize the widget in the app with respect to the center of the screen and not with respect to the common inferior left edge.

Now in the Python file, we have two widget classes, namely `MyW()` and `MyW1()`. It is easy to identify that `MyW()` is the class for the main widget because if we see the `e5App()` class when we build the class, it returns the `MyW()` class. We have been commonly using this class in our apps, but we focus on the second to last line where we create a reference to the `MyW1()` class, which is the layout widget, a widget like any other. Therefore, we can add to the main widget, which is what we do in the last line of the `MyW()` class.

The `MyW1()` class is the definition of the layout widget. See how this class has the property reference as the `FloatLayout` widget. Another fact to emphasize is the last line of this class, where we give a size to our widget (as we can do for all widgets), but now this will affect all the widget inside this one.

There's more...

There is more to say about the `pos_hint` instruction: it actually admits two more pairs of keys. To understand this better, let's focus on the second button of the KV file in which we have `pos_hint: {'center_x':.1, 'center_y': .1}` where we are using the keys `center_x` and `center_y` to define the position with respect to the center of the widget. We can change it to `pos_hint: {'x':.1, 'y': .1}` to locate the widget with respect to the usual inferior left edge, or we can use `pos_hint: {'right':.1, 'top': .1}` to use the superior right edge as the reference.

Using FloatLayout

One of the most common layouts is **FloatLayout** because it allows us to place the children widgets with arbitrary locations and size. The current recipe will use these particularities of `FloatLayouts` to organize an app with three buttons, one near the inferior left edge, the other one at the center, and the last one at the superior right edge.

Getting ready

This recipe is related to the previous recipe, *Organizing with layouts*, so it is important to read it and compare it with this recipe. The main difference is how the root widget is now the layout by itself.

How to do it...

In this recipe, we use the following steps to achieve the final goal:

1. In the KV file, define three buttons and set the `size_hint` and `pos_hint` properties:

   ```
   <MyW>:
       Button:
   ```

```
        id: label1
        size_hint: .2, .2
        pos_hint: {'center_x':.5, 'center_y': .5}
        text: 'B2'
    Button:
        id: label2
        size_hint: .1, .1
        pos_hint: {'x':.1, 'y': .1}
        text: 'B1'
    Button:
        id: label3
        size_hint: .1, .1
        pos_hint: {'x':.9, 'y': .9}
        text: 'B3'
```

2. In the Python file, import `FloatLayout`.

3. As shown here, define the class for the rule in the KV file with `FloatLayout` property:

```
import kivy

from kivy.app import App
from kivy.uix.widget import Widget
from kivy.uix.floatlayout import FloatLayout

class MyW(FloatLayout):
    pass

class e6App(App):
    def build(self):
        return MyW()

if __name__ == '__main__':
    e6App().run()
```

How it works...

In the KV file, we have to note that we are positioning the last two buttons to the last button with respect to the inferior left edge, and it should be located exactly at the limit of the app to show how it will conserve its position when the user changes the size of the window.

Now in the Python code, the root widget is the `FloatLayout` property. This is what creates the magic in the resizing effect, always keeping the positions visible in the app even though button B3 has position in the limit of window as is shown the following two figures.

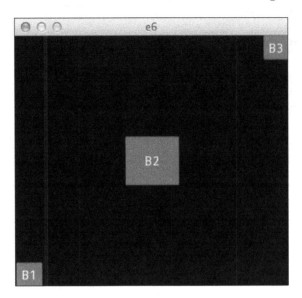

The preceding image shows the regular size of the app.

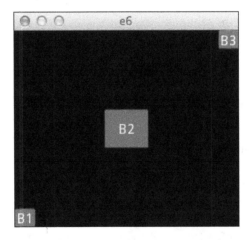

In the preceding image, you can see the size of the application has been decreased by the user.

There's more...

Something to clear about layouts is that it is difficult to make complete use of the KV file as we do in other widgets. You will probably need to import at least one layout; child layouts could be defined in the KV file. So it is very common to use `FloatLayout` as the root layout.

See also

If you want to know more about the nested layout, then see the upcoming recipes in this chapter.

Using BoxLayout

Now, we are going to introduce another layout widget named **BoxLayout**. Its name is a reference to the heap boxes where the boxes are the child widgets. To illustrate this, we will make a vertical heap of three buttons in this recipe.

Getting ready

You should be familiar with the widget tree abstraction, and it is important to check the recipes about the tree in this chapter.

How to do it...

We will need a KV file to set `BoxLayout` and a Python file to add the `BoxLayout` widget to our app. Follow the next steps:

1. In the KV file, define a `BoxLayout` widget and set the `size_hint` and orientation properties.

2. As children of the `BoxLayout`:

```
<MyW>:
    BoxLayout:
        size_hint: 0.5,0.5
        orientation: 'vertical'
        Button:
            id: label1
            text: 'B1'
        Button:
            id: label2
            text: 'B2'
        Button:
            id: label3
            text: 'B3'
```

3. In the Python file, import `FloatLayout`.

4. As shown here, define the class for the rule in the KV file with the `FloatLayout` property:

```
import kivy

from kivy.app import App
from kivy.uix.floatlayout import FloatLayout

class MyW(FloatLayout):
    pass

class e7App(App):
    def build(self):
        return MyW()

if __name__ == '__main__':
    e7App().run()
```

How it works...

Note how we are adding a `BoxLayout` widget in our rule `<MyW>`, as we do in any other widget. This widget has two properties, namely the `size_hint` and orientation properties. We know the first one well, but it is important to see how it is honored by the `BoxLayout` property as any other widget. The orientation gives the heap orientation, vertical or horizontal. The `BoxLayout` widget has three button children. Note how, in the following image, the first defined button is at the top of the heap.

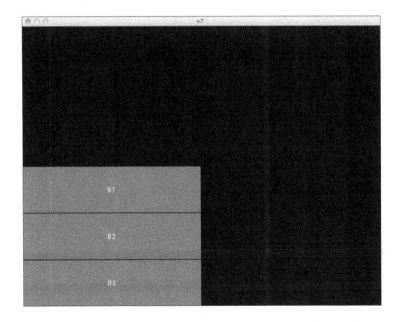

Let's see how the Python code is the same as the code in previous recipe where we are using the `FloatLayout` as root widget and we do not need to import the `BoxLayout`.

There's more...

The `BoxLayout` widget admits two more properties, spacing and padding:

- ▸ spacing gives the spaces between the children in pixels
- ▸ padding gives an empty border to the `BoxLayout`

Using GridLayout

`GridLayout` is the way to organize the child widgets in a table. In this recipe, we will organize four buttons in a 2x2 grid.

How to do it...

Again we will use the KV file to set the widgets and the Python file to set the layout. To complete the recipe:

1. In the KV file, provide the number of columns and rows with column and row properties.

2. Also, define four buttons using the following code:

```
<MyW>:
    cols: 2
    rows: 2
    Button:
        id: label1
        text: 'B1'
    Button:
        id: label2
        text: 'B2'
    Button:
        id: label3
        text: 'B3'
    Button:
        id: label4
        text: 'B4'
```

3. In the Python file, import `GridLayout`.

4. Define the root class as `GridLayout`. Use the following code to do that:

```
import kivy

from kivy.app import App
from kivy.uix.gridlayout import GridLayout

class MyW(GridLayout):
    pass

class e8App(App):
    def build(self):
        return MyW()

if __name__ == '__main__':
    e8App().run()
```

How it works...

In the KV file, we are using the row and column properties, which give the size of the grid. Also we have defined the four buttons. Note how they do not need the size or `size_hint` property, because they will cover the entire space available.

Now, Python knows that we are using `GridLayout` because the root class is referenced as `GridLayout`.

There's more...

There is something that we could see happening if we added an additional button in this recipe—the fifth button in the KV file:

```
Button:
    id: label5
    text: 'B5'
```

Kivy will respect the grid provided by us, so it will be added, as there was no layout.

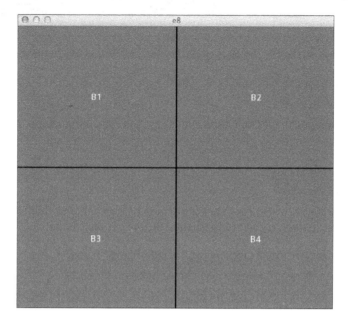

Here is the image of the app with four buttons, and the following is the image of the app with five buttons.

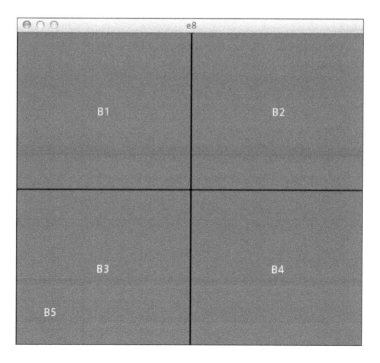

Using StackLayout

The `StackLayout` widget refers to stacking boxes, so it stacks the widgets one over another In this recipe, we will stack four buttons of different sizes to see the behavior of the layout.

Getting ready

In this recipe, we will use the Python code similar to the code in the recipe *Using the BoxLayout*. I would recommend you to go through the preceding recipe.

How to do it...

In this recipe, we will use the KV file to set the `StackLayout` and its children. The Python file is a code that we have been using in the layouts. Follow the next steps:

1. In the KV file, define a `StackLayout` child widget.

2. Using the orientation property, give an orientation for stacking.

3. Define a button as a child of the `StackLayout` widget, which should be 50 percent of the `StackLayout` widget's size.

4. Using the following code, define four additional buttons as children of the `StackLayout`, each of 25 percent of `StackLayout`'s size:

```
<MyW>:
    StackLayout:
        orientation: 'bt-lr'
        Button:
            id: label1
            size_hint: .5, .5
            text: 'B1'
        Button:
            id: label2
            size_hint: .25, .25
            text: 'B2'
        Button:
            id: label3
            size_hint: .25, .25
            text: 'B3'
        Button:
            id: label4
            size_hint: .25, .25
            text: 'B4'
```

5. In the Python file, import the `FloatLayout`.

6. Define the class for the rule in the KV file with `FloatLayout` property as shown here:

```
import kivy

from kivy.app import App
from kivy.uix.floatlayout import FloatLayout

class MyW(FloatLayout):
    pass

class e9App(App):
    def build(self):
        return MyW()

if __name__ == '__main__':
    e9App().run()
```

How it works...

For this layout, the most relevant thing is the property orientation that provides the notion of how the children have to be stacked. In the third line of the KV code, we set the orientation to `bt-lr` that means that the children will be stacked from bottom to up and left to right. Something to note is how the size of the child widgets is a relevant factor for this widget because it will only accommodate the widgets that fit in the app screen. Any other widget will not be shown, and the `StackLayout` respects the order in which the children appear in the KV file.

There's more...

The orientation property for the `StackLayout` gives us some freedom for child stacking. Remember the third line in the KV file:

```
orientation: 'bt-lr'
```

Here the stacking is from bottom to top, and when the maximum space in the vertical range is filled, the layout makes a new pile at the right to the first pile. If we want to make the stacking horizontally first, just swipe from `bt-lr` to `lr-bt`. Also, you can play with the different combinations, such as top, bottom, left, and right, as in the following images.

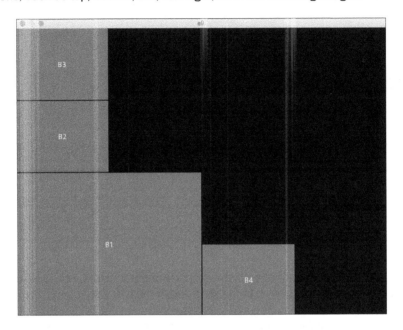

The preceding figure shows a `bt-lr` stacking.

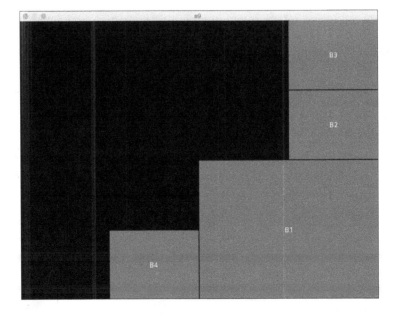

The preceding figure shows a `bt-rl` stacking.

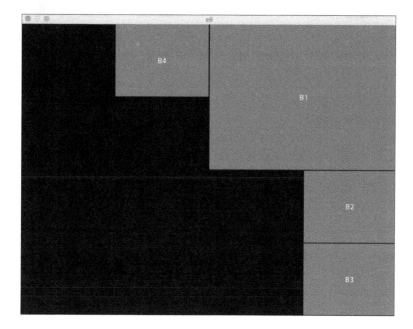

The preceding figure shows a `tb-rl` stacking.

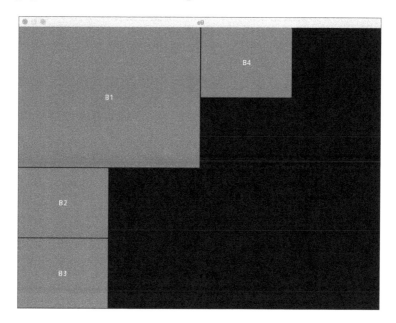

The preceding figure shows a `tb-lr` stacking.

Using RelativeLayout

RelativeLayout is a self-contained layout where the positions are relative to the layout and not with the app window. In this recipe, we will localize two buttons in RelativeLayout, which will be a child of FloatLayout.

Getting ready

The RelativeLayout is similar to the FloatLayout; thus, to spot the difference, it is advisable to go through the *Using FloatLayout* recipe.

How to do it...

To complete the recipe, perform the following steps:

1. In the KV file, define two buttons with different positions using the following code:

```
<MyW1>:
    Button:
        id: label1
        size_hint: .2, .2
        pos: 150, 150
        text: 'B1'
    Button:
        id: label2
        size_hint: .1, .1
        pos: 30, 30
        text: 'B2'
```

2. In the Python file, define a class as a RelativeLayout reference for the rule of the KV file.

3. Set size and position for the layout.

4. As shown here, define a subclass of FloatLayout and add the RelativeLayout as a child.

```
import kivy

from kivy.app import App
from kivy.uix.relativelayout import RelativeLayout
from kivy.uix.floatlayout import FloatLayout

class MyW1(RelativeLayout):
    def __init__(self, **kwargs):
        super(MyW1, self).__init__(**kwargs)
        self.size=(300,300)
```

```
            self.pos=(300,0)

    class MyW(FloatLayout):
        def __init__(self, **kwargs):
            super(MyW, self).__init__(**kwargs)
            self.MyW1_name=MyW1()
            self.add_widget(self.MyW1_name)

    class e10App(App):
        def build(self):
            return MyW()

    if __name__ == '__main__':
        e10App().run()
```

How it works...

The `RelativeLayout` is described by the `MyW1` class. Let's see how do we do that with the following instruction:

```
self.pos=(300,0)
```

We are placing the widget far from the origin, and the button with the `label1` ID has `pos= 150, 150`, but this is with respect to the position of the `RelativeLayout` taking the origin as (300,0) point. The output is shown in the following image.

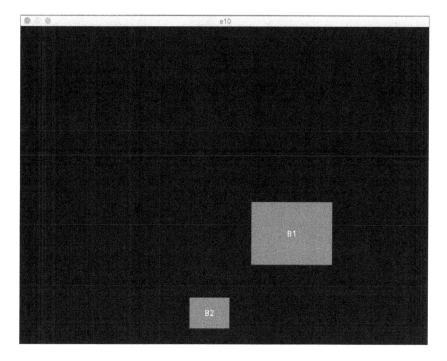

Using AnchorLayout

AnchorLayout aligns the children to a border or center. In this recipe, we will learn to align two buttons in a border.

How to do it...

In this recipe, follow the next steps:

1. In the KV file, provide the `anchor_x` and `anchor_y` properties.

2. Define two buttons using the following code:

```
<MyW>:
    anchor_x: 'right'
    anchor_y: 'bottom'
    Button:
        id: label1
        size_hint: .2, .2
        text: 'B1'
    Button:
        id: label2
        size_hint: .1, .1
        text: 'B2'
```

3. In the Python file, define a class as an `AnchorLayout` reference for the rule of the KV file using the following code:

```
import kivy

from kivy.app import App
from kivy.uix.anchorlayout import AnchorLayout from kivy.clock
import Clock

class MyW(AnchorLayout):
    pass
class e11App(App):
    def build(self):
        return MyW()

if __name__ == '__main__':
    e11App().run()
```

How it works...

The second and third lines of the KV file are the properties that are defined with respect to which border we will align the widgets. If we do not provide any of them, center will be selected by default. The anchor accepts the property padding, which we have already reviewed in *Using BoxLayout* recipe. In the following output, we can see how both the buttons are aligned with respect to the right-bottom edge:

Working with ActionBar

The `ActionBar` widget is like the popular Android's `ActionBar`. Here the children are stacked in horizontal and vertical groups such as menus. This recipe will use the `ActionBar` widget to organize eight buttons, and the bar will be the superior part of the app that has two buttons.

Getting ready

In this recipe, we need an icon such as the commonly used save icon. For this purpose, we will use the image `floppy.png`, which looks like:

How to do it...

Here, we will use a KV file to set and organize `ActionBar` and its children and the Python file to add `ActionBar` to our app. To complete the task, perform the following steps:

1. In the KV file, define the rule `<MyW>`.

2. In this rule, add the `ActionBar` widget.

3. In the `ActionBar` child, add a button with the `floppy.png` icon.

4. Add three more buttons.

5. Add three child buttons to `ActionGroup`.

6. Define another rule `<MyW>` with two buttons using the following code:

```
<MyW>:
    ActionBar:
        pos_hint: {'top':1}
        ActionView:
            use_separator: True
            ActionPrevious:
                title: 'Action Bar'
                with_previous: False
            ActionOverflow:
            ActionButton:
                text: 'Btn0'
                icon: 'floppy.png'
            ActionButton:
                text: 'Btn1'
```

```
                    ActionButton:
                         text: 'Btn2'
                    ActionButton:
                         text: 'Btn3'
                    ActionButton:
                         text: 'Btn4'
                    ActionGroup:
                         text: 'Group1'
                         ActionButton:
                              text: 'Btn5'
                         ActionButton:
                              text: 'Btn6'
                         ActionButton:
                              text: 'Btn7'
<MyW1>:
    Button:
        id: label1
        size_hint: .2, .2
        pos_hint: {'center_x':.5, 'center_y': .5}
        text: 'B1'
    Button:
        id: label2
        size_hint: .1, .1
        pos_hint: {'center_x':.1, 'center_y': .1}
        text: 'B2'
```

7. In the Python file, using the following code, define the two classes for the two rules of
    the KV file referenced as `FloatLayouts`:

```
import kivy

from kivy.app import App
from kivy.uix.floatlayout import FloatLayout

class MyW(FloatLayout):
    def __init__(self, **kwargs):
        super(MyW, self).__init__(**kwargs)
        self.add_widget(MyW1())

class MyW1(FloatLayout):
    pass

class e12App(App):
    def build(self):
```

```
        return MyW()

if __name__ == '__main__':
    e12App().run()
```

How it works...

Let's review the KV file in detail. The second line is where we are adding the action bar to the root widget. The third line gives the location of the bar on the screen: in this case it is the top. The fourth line starts with the description of the elements in the bar. In the seventh line, we provide the title of the action bar. The eighth line gives the option to select the use of the previous button or not. The previous button will help us return to the last screen of the app. The ninth line defines the actions when the bar overflows because if we do not declare any further option, it will use the default action. In the twelfth line, we are using an icon, which will be shown if the bar is not in an overflow state; in this case, the text will be shown. In the first twenty lines, we use a group that has three child buttons.

See also

If you want to know more about the transition of screens in the app, see the next chapter, *Graphics*.

5
Graphics – Canvas and Instructions

In this chapter, we will cover:

- ▶ Separating with the screen manager
- ▶ Using drawing instructions
- ▶ Using context instructions
- ▶ Working with manipulating instructions
- ▶ Rotating, translating, and scaling the canvas
- ▶ Modifying with multitouching
- ▶ Storing and retrieving the coordinate space context
- ▶ Introducing animations

Introduction

Graphics are an essential element in the Kivy philosophy and this is why each widget has graphical properties (even our app root widget). Canvas is used to represent the widget's graphics that you can see both as an unlimited drawing board and as a set of drawing instructions. We have two kinds of instructions, namely, vertex and context. The context instructions are not drawing anything, but they change as the result of the vertex instructions.

Instructions can also be arranged in two subsets according to the order in which they appear in the canvas. These subsets are the `canvas.before` and the `canvas.after` instruction groups. Their creation in our app depends on the user accesses.

The principal package used to work with graphics in Kivy is `kivy.graphics`, which is compatible with OpenGL ES 2.0 and has many rendering optimizations.

Separating with the screen manager

Its useful for a new app to have the opportunity to use more than one screen to organize our app content. These screens could be different from each other. The screen manager is the widget that permits this. In this recipe, we will develop an app that has two screens with different widgets in each one.

Getting ready

The readers must be aware and familiar with the concepts of the previous chapter as we use them to create this app. Particularly, the recipe *Using Swappable Widgets* in *Chapter 4, Widgets*.

How to do it...

We are going to create a KV code where we define and set the screen manager. Also, we will have a Python code where we will create the two screens that will be part of the screen manager. To complete the task, follow these steps:

1. In the KV file, import the `screenmanager` package.

2. Define the rule for the root widget.

3. Define `BoxLayout` for the buttons.

4. Define the `screenmanager` widget, with the property transition.

5. Define a new rule that controls the buttons, which change the screens:

```
#: import sm1 kivy.uix.screenmanager

<MyW>:
    orientation: 'vertical'
    BoxLayout:
        size_hint_y: None
        height: 30
        id: buttons
    ScreenManager:
        id: sm
        transition: sm1.WipeTransition()

<MButton>:
    on_press: app.root.ids.sm.current = self.text
```

6. In the Python file, import the usual package to use Kivy.

7. Also, import the screen manager package.

8. Define the class for the buttons' rules.

9. Define the class for the root widget.

10. In the __init__() method, create and add two screens to the root widget with different content for each one.

11. With the help of the following code, add two buttons that will help you switch between the two screens:

```
from kivy.app import App
from kivy.lang import Builder
from kivy.uix.label import Label
from kivy.uix.button import Button
from kivy.uix.boxlayout import BoxLayout
from kivy.uix.screenmanager import Screen

class MButton(Button):
    pass

class MyW(BoxLayout):
    def __init__(self, **kwargs):
        super(MyW, self).__init__(**kwargs)

        s = Screen(name="Hello1")
        s.add_widget(Label(text="src1"))
        self.ids.sm.add_widget(s)

        s = Screen(name="Hello2")
        s.add_widget(Label(text="src2"))
        self.ids.sm.add_widget(s)

        self.ids.buttons.add_widget(MButton(
        text="Hello1"))
        self.ids.buttons.add_widget(MButton(
        text="Hello2"))


class e1App(App):

    def build(self):
        return MyW()

if __name__ == '__main__':
    e1App().run()
```

How it works...

The KV code has a new relevant characteristic in the first line. There, we are importing a package to be used in the Kv language.

 Note that the difference between the usual method in Python—the token #—is necessary.

In the transition property of the `screenmanager` widget, we are calling a predefined transition that is in the imported package.

In the Python file, we are creating a screen with the line:

```
s = Screen(name="Hello1")
```

The name attribute is used to identify this specific screen. In the next line, we add widgets to the screen. In this case, it's a simple label, but we can add whatever is necessary:

```
s.add_widget(Label(text="src1"))
```

We have the next line:

```
self.ids.sm.add_widget(s)
```

This is where we add the screen to our `screenmanager` widget. In this recipe, we repeated this process for the second screen. The magic of the transitions between the screen is done with the help of the two buttons added to the `BoxLayout` which is defined in the KV file in the following lines:

```
self.ids.buttons.add_widget(MButton(text="Hello1"))
self.ids.buttons.add_widget(MButton(text="Hello2"))
```

There's more...

Kivy has more transitions available for the `screenmanager` widget, and some of them are `SlideTransition()`, `SwapTransition()`, `FadeTransition()`, and `FallOutTransition`. If you want to play with them, just change the tenth line in the KV file as:

```
transition: sm1.SlideTransition()
```

Using drawing instructions

Let's start to create some new graphics. In a visual app, astonishing graphics are fundamentals. This recipe will create some basic geometric shapes.

Getting ready

This recipe uses the OpenGL philosophy about drawing; if you are not familiar with this, you have to keep in mind that the drawing of geometric shapes is based on the mathematical knowledge behind them. For example, the triangle needs three points to be drawn, but not any three points can draw a triangle.

How to do it...

In this recipe, in the KV file, we will be adding four drawing instructions to the root widget canvas, and we will have a simple Python file for our app. To complete the recipe, follow these steps:

1. In the KV file, define the rule for the root widget.
2. Define the canvas property for the root widget.
3. Add the drawing instructions for an ellipse.
4. Add the drawing instructions for a rectangle.
5. Add the drawing instructions for a triangle.
6. Add the drawing instructions for a line:

```
<MyW>:
    canvas:
        Ellipse:
            pos: 0,0
            size: 50,50
        Rectangle:
            pos: 100,0
            size: 50,50
        Triangle:
            points: 200,0,250,50,250,0
        Line:
            points: 300,0,350,300
```

7. Use the usual Python file for one widget app:

```
import kivy
from kivy.app import App
from kivy.uix.widget import Widget

class MyW(Widget):
    pass

class e2App(App):
    def build(self):
        return MyW()

if __name__ == '__main__':
    e2App().run()
```

How it works...

The canvas represents a property of the widgets in the KV file. We can see which root widget has the canvas property where we can add our drawing instructions. In the third line of the KV file, we are adding an ellipse to the canvas of the root widget. You can see how the ellipse uses the traditional `pos` and `size` properties in the usual format (*X, Y*) as in the Cartesian plane. Similarly, we can add a rectangle to the canvas. The triangle is quite different; we have to provide three vertices to draw the geometric shape. The points in the line should be as follows:

```
points: 200,0,250,50,250,0
```

They are distributed in a particular order wherein the first pair of numbers is the first pair of vertices, the second pair of numbers is the second pair of vertices, and so on. In the same sense, the string with a format *X1, Y1, X2, Y2, X3, Y3* is used for the `points` property. The line shape is similar, but a line needs only two points to be defined, so we use the string *X1, Y1, X2, Y2*.

There's more...

This recipe shows a very common case where we are drawing in the background of the app, but as in the Kivy philosophy, every widget has the canvas property, so you can draw over any widget. For example, let's say that we want to make the same four shapes over a button. For this, simply change the reference of the class `MyW()`:

```
class MyW(Widget):
```

From a widget to a button:

```
class MyW(Button):
```

This draws the same figure over a button.

Using context instructions

This recipe brings colors to our apps. As we said, the context instructions are those that do not draw but give context to the canvas. The recipe will give color to some geometric shapes.

Getting ready

The last recipe is related to this recipe. So, it should be useful to compare them because you will better understand the difference between the context and drawing instructions with practice. Also, we will use different color models, such as RGB.

How to do it...

Here, we are going to use a simple Python file in our app and concentrate on the KV file, which will have context and drawing instructions to generate the graphics in the app. To complete the recipe, follow these steps:

1. In the KV file, define the rule for the root widget.
2. Define the canvas property for the root widget.
3. Add the drawing instructions for an ellipse.
4. Add the context instructions for a color in RGB.
5. Add the drawing instructions for a rectangle.
6. Add the drawing instructions for a triangle.
7. Add the context instructions for a color in RGBA.
8. Add the drawing instructions for a line:

```
<MyW>:
    canvas:
        Ellipse:
            pos: 0,0
            size: 50,50
        Color:
            rgb: 1, 1, 0
        Rectangle:
            pos: 100,0
```

```
                    size: 50,50
                Triangle:
                    points: 200,0,250,50,250,0
                Color:
                    rgba: 0, 1, 0, .5
                Line:
                    points: 300,0,350,300
```

9. Use the usual Python file for one widget app:

```
import kivy
from kivy.app import App
from kivy.uix.widget import Widget

class MyW(Widget):
    pass

class e3App(App):
    def build(self):
        return MyW()

if __name__ == '__main__':
        e3App().run()
```

How it works...

The KV file now has both kinds of instructions, vertex, and context. The first shape added is the ellipse; so far, we are not doing anything differently, and we know that we will have the same non-color figure of the last recipe. In the next line, we have:

```
Color:
    rgb: 1, 1, 0
```

Here, we have given a color to the canvas, which means that, from now, all the new drawings will be of that selected color. In this case, it is yellow because we are using the RGB color model. Then, we add the triangle and the rectangle, which will be yellow, so we said that context instructions do not draw but modify the vertex results. The following is the next set of code:

```
Color:
    rgba: 0, 1, 0, .5
```

These lines will change the canvas to a lighter green color, and so the next vertex will be of the same color. Similar to RGB, we can use RGBA just by adding an opacity factor, which is indicated by the last number.

There's more...

To add color we can use not only RGB, but also HSV: hue—H, saturation—S, opacity—A. Using the lines as:

```
Color:
    hsv: 0, 1, 1
a: .5
h: .5
s: .5
```

Working with manipulating instructions

Sometimes, we want to change or update the look of the canvas. This kind of instruction is what we call a manipulating instruction. This recipe will demonstrate the use of these instructions with the help of an ellipse, which could change its size with the change of the screen size without a layout.

Getting ready

We are going to work with a predefined geometric shape in this recipe. You could find a clearer panorama if you had read the second recipe in this chapter. Also, we will trigger an event in the recipe, so you should be clear about *Chapter 3, Events,* and specifically the recipe *Creating custom events.*

How to do it...

We will just need a Python file to complete the task in the class of the root widget, and we will use the manipulating instructions by following these steps:

1. Import the usual Kivy package.
2. Import the ellipse.
3. Define the class for the root widget.
4. Draw the ellipse in the center of the app.
5. Bind the `pos` and `size` with the method `update_rect()`.

6. Define the method `update_rect()` to update the ellipse's pos and size:

```
import kivy

from kivy.app import App
from kivy.uix.widget import Widget
from kivy.graphics import Ellipse

class MyW(Widget):

    def __init__(self, **kwargs):
        super(MyW, self).__init__(**kwargs)
        with self.canvas:
            self.rect = Ellipse(pos=self.pos, size=(10,10))

        self.bind(pos=self.update_rect)
        self.bind(size=self.update_rect)

    def update_rect(self, *args):
        self.rect.pos = self.pos
        self.rect.size = self.size

class e4App(App):
    def build(self):
        return MyW()

if __name__ == '__main__':
    e4App().run()
```

How it works...

The first three lines are standard for working with Kivy. The fourth line is important because we are defining the ellipse in the Python code, so here it is necessary to import the ellipse widget. We have the eighth and ninth lines:

```
with self.canvas:
    self.rect = Ellipse(pos=self.pos, size=(10,10))
```

We are defining the ellipse in the canvas. Let's note how in Kivy, canvas supports the `with` statement. It permits all successive drawing commands that are properly indented to modify this canvas. Also, the statement makes sure that, after our drawing, the internal state can be cleaned up properly. The tenth and eleventh lines are:

```
self.bind(pos=self.update_rect)
self.bind(size=self.update_rect)
```

They are defining an action trigger, so any time that the position or the size of the root widget is changed, the `update_rect()` method is called. The twelfth line defines the `update_rect()` method, and the thirteenth line updates the position of the `rect` object (in this case, the ellipse) with the value of the root widget's position. The fourteenth line does the same with the size.

There's more...

Another manipulating instruction that we can use is the clean instruction. We can perform the same recipe just for cleaning the canvas. We just need to change the `update_rect()` method content to the following:

```
self.canvas.clear()
with self.canvas:
self.rect = Rectangle(pos=self.pos, size=self.size)
```

Rotating, translating, and scaling the canvas

The rotation, translation, and scaling canvas in Kivy is relatively easy with the use of matrices. In this recipe, we will create a traditional button and rotate its canvas.

Getting ready

Again the mathematics are important in graphics, so we should at least do a Wikipedia check about the matrix concept to get a real sense about what is happening with the canvas.

How to do it...

For this recipe, follow these steps:

1. In the KV file, define the rule for the root widget.
2. Define a button with a label and a position.
3. In `canvas.before`, push the matrix onto the context's matrix stack.
4. Rotate the matrix 45 degrees.
5. Use the translate instruction to translate the matrix.

6. In `canvas.after,` pop the matrix from the context's matrix stack onto the model view:

```
<MyW>:
    Button:
        text: 'hello world'
        size_hint: None, None
        pos_hint: {'center_x': .5, 'center_y': .5}
        canvas.before:
            PushMatrix
            Rotate:
                angle: 45
                origin: self.center
            Translate:
                xy: self.center_x, self.center_y

        canvas.after:
            PopMatrix
```

7. Use the usual Python file for one widget app:

```
import kivy
from kivy.app import App
from kivy.uix.widget import Widget

class MyW(Widget):
    pass

class e5App(App):
    def build(self):
        return MyW()

if __name__ == '__main__':
    e5App().run()
```

How it works...

In the KV file, we have the usual definition of the root widget and a button with its position and its label. The newly introduced concept is the `canvas.before` statement with the line:

PushMatrix

Here, we are pushing the matrix of the model view onto the context's matrix stack with the intention of changing it. That is what we do with the following lines:

```
Rotate:
    angle: 45
    origin: self.center
Translate:
    xy: self.center_x, self.center_y
```

They rotate and translate the matrix. We re-establish the matrix with the two last lines of the file:

```
canvas.after:
    PopMatrix
```

We pop the matrix from the context's matrix stack onto the model view.

There's more...

There are other functions that we can use to change the matrix, which are as follows:

- **identity()**: This resets the matrix to the identity matrix (in place)
- **inverse()**: This returns the inverse of the matrix as a new matrix
- **look_at()**: This returns a new `look_at` matrix (similar to gluLookAt)
- **multiply()**: This multiplies the given matrix with self (from the left)
- **normal_matrix()**: This computes the normal matrix, which is the inverse transpose of the top left 3x3 model view matrix that is used to transform normals into eye/camera space
- **perspective()**:This creates a perspective matrix (in place)
- **project()**: This projects a point from a 3D space into a 2D viewport.
- **scale()**:This scales the current matrix by the specified factors over each dimension (in place)
- **transpose()**:This returns the transposed matrix as a new matrix

A fun fact to mention is that these functions are working with real matrices, and this is why the GPUs are now so important, and which will help us in mathematics computations.

Modifying with multitouching

A modern use of the gestures and touches is to change the graphics of the app. What things such as pinch to zoom actually do is to scale the canvas of a widget. In this recipe, we will use the scatter widget that Kivy has for these purposes.

Getting ready

The magic of this kind of widget is understood well in the Kivy widgets tree. You could check *Chapter 4*, *Widgets* in the recipe *Manipulating the widget tree*.

How to do it...

You will use a Python file where you will add and set the scatter widget to the root widget. To complete the task, follow these steps:

1. In the Python file, import the usual packages to work with Kivy.

2. Import the `Scatter` widget.

3. Define a class for the root widget.

4. Create a simple button with a label.

5. Create the scatter widget.

6. Add the button to the scatter widget.

7. Add the scatter widget to the root widget as follows:

```python
import kivy

from kivy.app import App
from kivy.uix.widget import Widget
from kivy.uix.button import Button
from kivy.uix.scatter import Scatter

class MyW(Widget):
    def __init__(self, **kwargs):
        super(MyW, self).__init__(**kwargs)
        but1 = Button(text='hello')
        scatter = Scatter(size=(400, 400), size_hint=(None,
        None))
        scatter.add_widget(but1)
        self.add_widget(scatter)
```

```
class e6App(App):
    def build(self):
        return MyW()


if __name__ == '__main__':
    e6App().run()
```

How it works...

In the root widget class, we are defining the scatter widget with its size and position. The scatter is used to build interactive widgets that can be translated, rotated, and scaled with two or more fingers on a multitouch system. We have the following line:

```
scatter.add_widget(but1)
```

We are giving the versatility of the scatter widget to the button, as it is now a child of the scatter widget. We have the following line:

```
self.add_widget(scatter)
```

This is where the scatter widget is added to the root widget. This addition should be done after all the widgets that we want to be part of the scatter have been already added to the scatter widget.

There's more...

There is also a layout called ScatterLayout, which permits to organization of all the widgets of an app under the scatter advantages. In contrast to a scatter, the layout favors the hint properties for the widgets as pos_hint. Basically, the ScatterLayout is implemented as a FloatLayout inside a scatter.

Also, we can use scatter in the Kv language like any other widget. For example, in the following code, we can get the same result with this recipe:

```
<MyW>:
    Scatter:
        size: 400,400
        Button:
            size: 50,50
            text: 'Hello'
```

Storing and retrieving the coordinate space context

The graphical environment in Kivy uses a coordinate space to locate the content. In this recipe, we will take a look at how to work with the coordinate space. This recipe will define a vector and make some basic operations with it.

Getting ready

Now we are going to use the mathematical concept of vectors. You will get a better understanding of this recipe if you have the concept clear. Read the Wikipedia about it, a good start point. The implementation is made on top of a Python list, so it is important to have a good understanding of that concept too.

How to do it...

In this recipe, we will work directly with Python to show the possibilities of the vectors in Kivy, for which we will use the common vector operations.

1. First, let's define a vector:

   ```
   v = Vector(82, 34)
   ```

2. Now if we want to retrieve the coordinate from a widget, we use:

   ```
   w = widget.pos
   ```

3. The sum of the last two defined vectors is given by:

   ```
   x = v + w
   ```

4. The product of those vectors is given by:

   ```
   y = v * w
   ```

5. The angle between the two vectors is given by:

   ```
   Vector(v).angle(w)
   ```

6. The distance between the two vectors is given by:

   ```
   Vector(v).distance(w)
   ```

7. The square distance is given by:

   ```
   Vector(v).distance2(w)
   ```

8. The dot product between vectors is given by:

   ```
   Vector(v).dot(w)
   ```

9. The length of a vector is given by:

   ```
   Vector(v).length()
   ```

10. To normalize a vector, we use:

    ```
    Vector(v).normalize()
    ```

11. To rotate the vector, we use:

    ```
    Vector(v).rotate(45)
    ```

12. To get just one component, we use:

    ```
    v.x
    ```

Introducing animations

The use of graphics opens up a diversity of options: one of them is animations. Kivy is useful for this task. For this recipe, we will develop a simple animation of a button where, if you touch it, the animation is performed.

Getting ready

Animations are a natural extension of the graphics concepts. It is good to have those concepts clear so, as recommended, you should read the previous recipes of this chapter.

How to do it...

Here we are going to use KV file where we set the button to perform the animation that will be defined in the Python file as a method of the root widget class. For this, follow these steps:

1. In the KV file, define the rule for the root widget.
2. Add a button to the root widget.
3. Call the `root.animate()` method in the `on_press` property of the button:
   ```
   <MyW>:
       Button:
           id: button1
           text: 'Hello'
           on_press: root.animate(button1)
   ```
4. In the Python file, import the usual Kivy packages.
5. Also import the `Animation` package.
6. Define the root widget class.

7. Define the `animate()` method inside the root widget class.

8. In the method, provide the animation parameters.

9. Also declare the start statement as follows:

```
import kivy

from kivy.app import App
from kivy.uix.widget import Widget
from kivy.animation import Animation

class MyW(Widget):

    def animate(self, instance):
        animation = Animation(pos=(100, 100), t='out_bounce')
        animation += Animation(pos=(200, 100), t='out_bounce')
        animation &= Animation(size=(500, 500))
        animation += Animation(size=(100, 50))
        animation.start(instance)

class e8App(App):

    def build(self):
        return MyW()

if __name__ == '__main__':
    e8App().run()
```

How it works...

The KV code presents a traditional root widget with a button with an `on_press` event that will call the `animate()` method when the button is touched.

In the Python code, we have imported the usual Kivy packages with the addition of the animation package that will help us create the animation of the widget. In the root widget class, we have the method `animate()`, which will perform the animation. We have the following line:

```
animation = Animation(pos=(100, 100), t='out_bounce')
```

We have given directions for the animation: in a continuous movement the widget will move to a position (100,100). We have the following line:

```
animation += Animation(pos=(200, 100), t='out_bounce')
```

Now we have added another movement of the widget to the position (200,100). Let's note the use of the operator + to add sequential movements. Now see the following line:

```
animation &= Animation(size=(500, 500))
```

It is interesting because here we are performing a parallel action with respect to the last two lines: namely, they will be performed together in the animation and the token `&=` are creating a new thread in the animation. The preceding line changes the size of the widget. Now see the following line:

```
animation += Animation(size=(100, 50))
```

This also changes the size of the widget. We have the following line:

```
animation.start(instance)
```

This line will help in the animation. Let's note how the animation is applied to `instance` that is a parameter of the `animate()` method so that we can apply this animation to any widget we like.

There's more...

The function `Animation()` imported from the package `kivy.animation` has precisely three arguments:

- **duration or d**: This is a float data with a default value of *1*. It provides the duration of the animation in seconds.
- **transition or t**: This is a string or function. It provides a transition function for `animate` properties. It can be the name of a method from `AnimationTransition`.
- **step or s**: This is a float data with a default value of *1/60*. It provides the step in milliseconds of the animation.

See also

If you want to know more about animation in Kivy, you should read *Chapter 7, The API in Detail,* especially the *Working with Video* and *Working with Audio* recipes.

6
Advanced Graphics – Shaders and Rendering

In this chapter, we will cover:

- ▶ Using Carousel
- ▶ Creating and using Atlas
- ▶ Creating layouts
- ▶ Editing shaders
- ▶ Creating widgets
- ▶ Creating your own shader
- ▶ Rendering in a Framebuffer
- ▶ Optimizing graphics

Introduction

Graphics have a relevant position in the Kivy environment. So, we want to go deeper into the possibilities opened by the framework. The previous chapter gave us the necessary tools to create our own graphics and animations. However, now we will describe how to use advance features, that is, the inclusion of OpenGL code in our app. OpenGL gives the ability to use 3D graphics, and it processes graphics faster than we did in the previous chapter.

In this spirit, we will review the creation of widgets and layouts, and how graphics are important for them.

We will look at a recipe of the buffering technique to render our graphics, and we will detail some good practices to code our graphical instructions. Let's start having a look at the `Carousel` widget, which opens the possibility of handling more graphics than what fit in our app.

Using Carousel

The `Carousel` widget is an advanced way to present pictures, which is already present in modern apps. This is because it permits to display a large number of pictures in a helpful way for when the user wants to search for a particular one. In this recipe, we will create an app with the Carousel widget where the user will navigate between three pictures. They will look like the following:

If you drag the image to the right, you will see this next image:

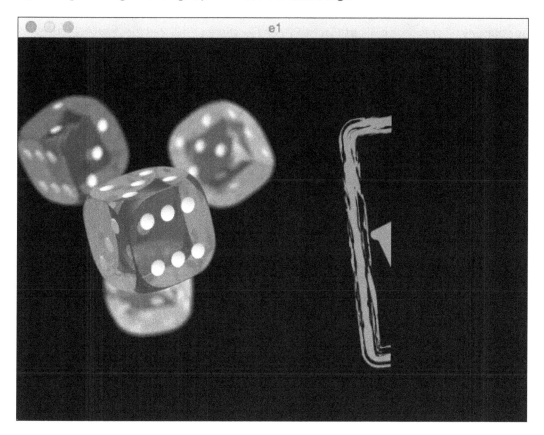

Getting ready

In order to start this recipe, it is necessary to have three different pictures in standard formats (that is, PNG or JPEG). We have to rename them as f0.png, f1.png, and f2.png, or with the .jpg extension if it is appropriate.

How to do it...

To complete this recipe, we will use just a Python file where we will call the Carousel widget and set it up to display our pictures. Follow these steps:

1. Import the usual `kivy` packages.
2. Import the `Factory` package.
3. Import the `Carousel` widget.
4. Define the root `widget` class.
5. In the `__init__()` method, call the Carousel widget.
6. Call the three pictures and add them to the Carousel.
7. Add the Carousel to the root widget:

```python
import kivy
kivy.require('1.9.0') # Code tested in this version!
from kivy.app import App
from kivy.uix.widget import Widget
from kivy.factory import Factory
from kivy.uix.carousel import Carousel

class MyW(Widget):
    def __init__(self, **kwargs):
        super(MyW, self).__init__(**kwargs)
        carousel = Carousel(direction='right')
        for i in range(3):
            src = "f%d.png" % i
            image = Factory.AsyncImage(source=src,
            allow_stretch=True)
            carousel.add_widget(image)
        self.add_widget(carousel)

class e1App(App):

    def build(self):
        return MyW()

if __name__ == '__main__':
    e1App().run()
```

How it works...

The Carousel seems to be a normal widget that organizes other widgets, but it has the particularity that it could arrange more widgets than the number of widgets that can actually fit into its area. This is why, we have two special considerations in the following line:

```
image = Factory.AsyncImage(source=src, allow_stretch=True)
```

The first consideration is the `Factory` instruction, which helps not to reserve more memory than necessary. You could directly use the `AsyncImage()` method, but this would create a call by each image, and if we have a bunch of them, this approach will generate more data than we want. The second consideration is the use of the `AsyncImage()` method instead of the `Image()` method; this is because the `AsyncImage()` method does an asynchronous loading of the image preventing if some image cannot be loaded, the app will be blocked. This is achieved by doing the image retrieve as a background process.

There's more...

Actually, we can use this widget not only to organize images but also any widget. For instance, let's add a button to our Carousel just with the line:

```
carousel.add_widget(Button(text='Hi'))
```

As seen before, this is the line where we add the Carousel widget to the root widget. Also, it is necessary to import the `button` widget adding the line someplace after the second line:

```
from kivy.uix.button import Button
```

Creating and using Atlas

Atlas is a useful tool for any app because it permits the condensing of all the pictures that we are going to use in the app in just two simple files. Atlas has the advantage that the app only needs to load just one image file, which is less error susceptible, and also it is cheaper in resource usage than loading several images, especially if it's done over the Web. The Atlas area is used a lot in games for rendering. This recipe will use a button that will swap the background images when clicked.

Getting ready

We will need three different pictures in standard formats (that is, PNG or JPEG). With these pictures, we will create an Atlas. From the terminal, go to the directory where the pictures are. There, use the instruction:

```
$ python -m kivy.atlasmyatlas 2065 *.png
```

We create an Atlas file with the name `myatlas`. The number *2065* is the size of the Atlas, which is supposed to be square, in this case 2065x2065 pixels. We should carefully decide this number. We should consider the total size of the images we are including. If we're just packing in three 128x128 images, an Atlas size of 2065x2065 is inefficient; in this case 384x384 is better.

When we run the instruction, it generates two files (`myatlas.atlas` and `myatlas-0.png`), which should be copied into the same directory as our app Python file.

How to do it...

Now, we will use a Python file to use the previously created Atlas. The app will have only a button that changes its background when pressed. To complete the task, follow these steps:

1. Import the usual Kivy packages.

2. Define the __init__() class for the root widget.

3. In this class, define a button that uses two images from Atlas.

4. Add the `button` to the root widget.

```python
import kivy
kivy.require('1.9.0') # Code tested in this version!
from kivy.app import App
from kivy.uix.widget import Widget
from kivy.uix.button import Button

class MyW(Widget):
    def __init__(self, **kwargs):
        super(MyW, self).__init__(**kwargs)
        a = Button(size=(200,200),
        background_normal='atlas://myatlas/f1',
        background_down='atlas://myatlas/f2')
        self.add_widget(a)

class e2App(App):

    def build(self):
        return MyW()

if __name__ == '__main__':
    e2App().run()
```

How it works...

In this very usual Python code, we are using the advantages of the Atlas file; specifically, consider the following line:

```
a = Button(size=(200,200),background_normal='atlas://myatlas/f1',
background_down='atlas://myatlas/f2')
```

Here, we have the reference `atlas://myatlas/f1` and `atlas://myatlas/f2`, which calls two of the three images that are in the Atlas. Note how `myatlas` corresponds to the name of the Atlas that we are using and `f1` corresponds to the tag in the Atlas for that image. The tag corresponds to the original image's original name without the extension.

Creating layouts

Layout widgets are useful to organize the widgets in our app, but we can get more benefits from them if we include some graphics in them. In this recipe, we will add a background to a layout.

Getting ready

We are going to work with layouts in this recipe, so you should have cleared the concepts behind them. It is recommended that you read the recipe *Organizing with layouts* in *Chapter 4, Widgets*. We will also use the three images from the first recipe of this chapter.

How to do it...

In this recipe, we are going to use a KV file to define our new layout and basic Python to execute our app. To complete the recipe, perform the following steps:

1. In the KV file, define a widget named `CustomLayout`.
2. Give a yellow rectangle layout to the canvas.
3. Define another widget with our usual `MyW`.
4. Call `CustomLayout`.
5. Put one of the images at the center of the layout.
6. Put another image out side of the layout.
7. Call `CustomLayout` again.

8. Put one of the images at the center of the layout:

```
<CustomLayout>:
    canvas.before:
        Color:
            rgba: 1, 1, 0, 1
        Rectangle:
            pos: self.pos
            size: self.size
<MyW>:
    CustomLayout:
        AsyncImage:
            source: 'f1.png'
            size_hint: 1, .5
            pos_hint: {'center_x':.5, 'center_y': .5}
    AsyncImage:
        source: 'f0.png'
    CustomLayout:
        AsyncImage:
            source: 'f2.png'
            size_hint: 1, .5
            pos_hint: {'center_x':.5, 'center_y': .5}
```

9. In the Python file, import the usual packages.

10. Import `FloatLayout` and `BoxLayout`.

11. Define the class `MyW` as the `BoxLayout` instance.

12. Define the class `CustomLayout` as the `FloatLayout` instance:

```
import kivy
kivy.require('1.9.0') # Code tested in this version!
from kivy.app import App
from kivy.uix.floatlayout import FloatLayout
from kivy.uix.boxlayout import BoxLayout

class MyW(BoxLayout):
    pass

class CustomLayout(FloatLayout):
    pass

class e3App(App):
    def build(self):
        return MyW()

if __name__ == '__main__':
    e3App().run()
```

How it works...

In the KV file, we have defined two rules. The first rule provides graphics to our custom layout. The second rule organizes the widgets in our app. Let's note how we are already using our custom layout to arrange the widgets in the app.

Now, in the Python file, we have imported the `FloatLayout` and the `BoxLayout` packages. We have instanced the root widget class as `BoxLayout` and `CustomLayout` class as `FloatLayout` as follows:

```
classCustomLayout(FloatLayout):
    pass
```

This instance gives our `CustomLayout` the characteristics of a layout. We are using `FloatLayout` because it gives us more freedom to create our own layout.

Editing shaders

Kivy, of course, permits us to work with shaders. The shaders calculate rendering effects with the help of the GPU. In this recipe, we will use a predefined shader that we will load from a `glsl` file, which is the common extension of the **OpenGL Shading Language** (**GLSL**).

Getting ready

We are going to need a `glsl` file to work with in this recipe; there exist thousands free on the Web.

 A nice place to look is the site `http://www.iquilezles.org/apps/shadertoy/index2.html` where you could find your favorite.

Also, you should be familiar with some concepts about shaders, so you can start reading the Wikipedia article at `http://en.wikipedia.org/wiki/OpenGL_Shading_Language`.

How to do it...

In this recipe, we will use the KV, Python, and `glsl` files of our choice. In the KV file, we will provide the size and position of the shader in the app, and in the Python file, we will set the behavior of the shader. Let's follow the next steps:

1. Open the `glsl` file and add the next header after the `#endif` instruction:

```
/* Outputs from the vertex shader */
varying vec4 frag_color;
```

```
varying vec2 tex_coord0;
/* uniform texture samplers */
uniform sampler2D texture0;
```

2. In the KV file, define the `ShaderWidget` rule.

3. Add `canvas` for `color`, `pos`, and `size`:

```
<ShaderWidget>:
canvas:
    Color:
        rgb: 1, 0, 0
    Rectangle:
        pos: self.pos
        size: self.size
```

4. In the Python file, import the usual Kivy packages.

5. Also import the `RenderContext` and `StringProperty` packages.

6. Open and read the `glsl` file.

7. Define the `ShaderWidget` class instanced as `FloatLayout`.

8. Define the variable as `StringProperty`.

9. Define the `__init__()` class.

10. In this class, define the canvas as `RenderContex`.

11. Update the `updated_glsl()` method to *60* times per second.

12. Define the `on_fs()` method that will be triggered when the `fs` variable changes.

13. Change the context `shader` to the information in the `fs` variable.

14. Define the `updated_glsl()` method that will update `RenderContext`.

```
import kivy
kivy.require('1.9.0') # Code tested in this version!
from kivy.clock import Clock
from kivy.app import App
from kivy.uix.floatlayout import FloatLayout
from kivy.core.window import Window
from kivy.graphics import RenderContext
from kivy.properties import StringProperty


fo = open("e4.glsl", "r+")
our_shader = fo.read()

classShaderWidget(FloatLayout):
```

```
        fs = StringProperty(None)

        def __init__(self, **kwargs):

            self.canvas = RenderContext()
            super(ShaderWidget, self).__init__(**kwargs)
            Clock.schedule_interval(self.update_glsl, 1 / 60.)

        def on_fs(self, instance, value):
            shader = self.canvas.shader
            old_value = shader.fs
            shader.fs = value
            if not shader.success:
                shader.fs = old_value
                raise Exception('failed')

        def update_glsl(self, *largs):
            self.canvas['time'] = Clock.get_boottime()
            self.canvas['resolution'] = list(map(float,
            self.size))
            self.canvas['projection_mat'] =\
            Window.render_context['projection_mat']


    class e4App(App):
        def build(self):
            return ShaderWidget(fs=our_shader)

    if __name__ == '__main__':
        e4App().run()
```

How it works...

The `glsl` file has been edited to be used in our Kivy framework; this modification makes the connection between the `glsl` variables and the Kivy counterparts. In the case of the KV file, we give a color, size, and position to `ShaderWidget` that is actually independent of the `shader` that we use.

Now, in the following lines from Python file:

```
fo = open("e4.glsl", "r+")
our_shader = fo.read()
```

This is a complete read of the file, which is a typical pythonic way of reading files, as a whole. We assign the string to the `plasma_shader` variable. In the `ShaderWidget` method, we have the following:

```
fs = StringProperty(None)
```

This is the variable that will store the shader to be used. Note how we create a generic definition with the help of the `StringProperty()` method that we imported. In the `__init__()` method, we set up the time that the shader is updated in the following line:

```
Clock.schedule_interval(self.update_glsl, 1 / 60.)
```

The method `on_fs()` will make the change between the default Kivy shader and the shader we want. Remember that this callback will be performed when the `fs` variable is modified. We have the following line:

```
shader = self.canvas.shader
```

We make the reference of the actual shader of the widget to the `shader` variable. Consider the following line:

```
old_value = shader.fs
```

This is so that if something fails we have a record of the original shader. This line is what makes the change:

```
shader.fs = value
```

The next ones are the exception handling procedures. The `update_glsl()` method is the one that updates the shader. Finally, consider the line:

```
returnShaderWidget(fs=our_shader)
```

This is where we assign the shader that we read from the file to our `ShaderWidget` method.

There's more...

Actually, we have more than one kind of shader. The modification to the `glsl` file that we presented in this recipe is for the **fragment shader**, which is the shader that renders the pixels of the widget. We also can work with a vertex shader, but we should make a distinct modification to the `glsl` file after the `#endif` instruction as follows:

```
/* Outputs to the_fragmentshader */
varying vec4 frag_color;
varying vec2 tex_coord0;
/* vertex attributes */
attribute vec2     vPosition;
attribute vec2     vTexCoords0;
/* uniform variables */
uniform mat4 modelview_mat;
```

```
uniform mat4 projection_mat;
uniform vec4 color;
uniform float opacity;
```

The **vertex shaders** are those that update the vertex of the GPU instance, such as the pixels of the widget.

Creating widgets

Actually, this topic has been almost covered in the last chapters, but now we can give graphics to our widgets. The following recipe will create a widget where the user can create graphics ad lib. When the user performs a touch in the widget, the app will draw a yellow point, and if he maintains the touch and moves it, the app will draw a yellow path for the movement.

Getting ready

We are going to work with the touch directive in this recipe. It is useful to read *Differencing between Touch and Motion events* recipe in *Chapter 2, Input, Motion, and Touch*.

How to do it...

We are going to use just one Python file to complete the task where we will define the method of our created widget. Follow these steps of the recipe:

1. Import the usual Kivy packages.
2. Define the `MyWidget` class instanced as a widget.
3. Define the `on_touch_down()` callback for the class.
4. In the method, add `canvas`, `Color`, and `Ellipse` to the widget.
5. Also add the initial point of the line to be drawn.
6. Define the `on_touch_move()` callback.
7. Add more points to the line of step 5:

```
import kivy

from kivy.app import App
from kivy.uix.widget import Widget
from kivy.graphics import Color, Ellipse, Line

class MyWidget(Widget):
    defon_touch_down(self, touch):
        withself.canvas:
            Color(1, 1, 0)
```

```
        d = 30.
        Ellipse(pos=(touch.x - d / 2, touch.y - d / 2),
        size=(d, d))
        touch.ud['line'] = Line(points=(touch.x,
        touch.y))

    defon_touch_move(self, touch):
        touch.ud['line'].points += [touch.x, touch.y]

class e5App(App):

    def build(self):
        returnMyWidget()

if __name__ == '__main__':
    e5App().run()
```

How it works...

Note that the `MyWidget()` class is instanced as a widget which is what makes our class a valid widget for the Kivy framework. Probably, in the recipe, the most important line is:

`withself.canvas:`

This provides graphics to our specific widget. Another aspect to point out is what happens in the following line:

`touch.ud['line'].points += [touch.x, touch.y]`

Even though this is a different method from the `on_touch_down()` method, you do not need to call the canvas again because both methods occur one after the other.

See also

The further elements that you need to create your custom widget; you will find them in *Chapter 1*, *Kivy and the Kv language*, and *Chapter 7*, *The API in Detail*, of this book.

Creating your own shader

We have already worked with shaders in this chapter, but now we will work with our own shaders. To show this, we will create an app with only the `ShaderWidget`.

Getting ready

We will use the preceding recipe *Editing shaders* to complete this recipe. Particularly, we will use the `ShaderWidget` class implemented there.

How to do it...

We will need a KV file and a Python file in this recipe. The KV file gives the size and position to the `ShaderWidget`, and the Python file will have our shader. Now, follow these steps:

1. In the KV file, define the `ShaderWidget` rule.

2. Add `canvas` for `color`, `pos,` and `size`:

   ```
   <ShaderWidget>:
   canvas:
       Color:
           rgb: 1, 0, 0
       Rectangle:
           pos: self.pos
           size: self.size
   ```

3. In the Python file, import the usual Kivy packages.

4. Also import the `RenderContext` and `StringProperty` packages.

5. Define the header of `Our shader`.

6. Define `Our shader`.

7. Define `ShaderWidget`.

8. Call `ShaderWidget` with `Our shader`:

   ```
   import kivy
   kivy.require('1.9.0') # Code tested in this version!
   from kivy.clock import Clock
   from kivy.app import App
   from kivy.uix.floatlayout import FloatLayout
   from kivy.core.window import Window
   from kivy.graphics import RenderContext
   from kivy.properties import StringProperty

   # This header must be not changed, it contain the minimum
   information from Kivy.
   header = '''
   #ifdef GL_ES
   precision highp float;
   ```

```
            #endif
            /* Outputs from the vertex shader */
            varying vec4 frag_color;
            varying vec2 tex_coord0;
            /* uniform texture samplers */
            uniform sampler2D texture0;
            '''


            # Our shader
            our_shader = "$HEADER$" + '''
            uniform vec2 resolution;
            uniform float time;
            void main(void)
            {
                float x = gl_FragCoord.x;
                float y = gl_FragCoord.y;
                float mov0 =
                x+y+cos(sin(time)*2.)*100.+sin(x/100.)*1000.;
                float mov1 = y / resolution.y / 0.2 + time;
                float c1 = abs(sin(mov1+time));
                float c2 = abs(sin(c1+sin(mov0/1000.+time)));
                float c3 = abs(sin(x/1000.));
                gl_FragColor = vec4(c1,c2,c3,1.0);
            }
            '''


            class ShaderWidget(FloatLayout):

                fs = StringProperty(None)

                def __init__(self, **kwargs):
                    self.canvas = RenderContext()
                    super(ShaderWidget, self).__init__(**kwargs)
                    Clock.schedule_interval(self.update_glsl, 1 / 60.)

                def on_fs(self, instance, value):
                    shader = self.canvas.shader
                    old_value = shader.fs
                    shader.fs = value
                    if not shader.success:
                        shader.fs = old_value
                        raise Exception('failed')
```

```
def update_glsl(self, *largs):
    self.canvas['time'] = Clock.get_boottime()
    self.canvas['resolution'] = list(map(float,
    self.size))
    self.canvas['projection_mat'] =
    Window.render_context['projection_mat']


class e6App(App):
    def build(self):
        return ShaderWidget(fs=our_shader)

if __name__ == '__main__':
    e6App().run()
```

How it works...

Let's have a look at the Python file where the shader is defined. Note how we are not using a `glsl` file as in the previous recipe. We are creating a fragment shader, and this is why, we use the following header:

```
header = '''
#ifdef GL_ES
precisionhighp float;
#endif

/* Outputs from the vertex shader */
varying vec4 frag_color;
varying vec2 tex_coord0;
/* uniform texture samplers */
uniform sampler2D texture0;
'''
```

Remember that this header makes the connection between `glsl` and Kivy. The string that represents our shader is a concatenation of this header and the code that we use. In the next lines, we have:

```
our_shader = "$HEADER$" + '''
uniform vec2 resolution;
uniform float time;
void main(void)
{
float x = gl_FragCoord.x;
float y = gl_FragCoord.y;
float mov0 = x+y+cos(sin(time)*2.)*100.+sin(x/100.)*1000.;
```

```
float mov1 = y / resolution.y / 0.2 + time;
float c1 = abs(sin(mov1+time));
float c2 = abs(sin(c1+sin(mov0/1000.+time)));
float c3 = abs(sin(x/1000.));
gl_FragColor = vec4(c1,c2,c3,1.0);
}
'''
```

Note how the `gl_FragCoord` is an instruction that gets the coordinates of the pixels. The other lines are some calculations based on these retrieved coordinates and the time. Finally with the `gl_FragColor` instruction, we update the color of the pixel that is the object of this shader.

There's more...

Again, if we want to use a vertex shader, the header should be distinct. We have to use:

```
header = '''
#ifdef GL_ES
precisionhighp float;
#endif

/* Outputs from the vertex shader */
varying vec4 frag_color;
varying vec2 tex_coord0;
/* uniform texture samplers */
uniform sampler2D texture0;
```

See also

If you want to know more about shaders, you can refer to the book *OpenGL 4 Shading Language Cookbook* by David Wolff.

Rendering in a Framebuffer

The Framebuffer represents a helpful tool for the graphical content of Kivy. It is an offscreen tool where we can draw any complex set of instructions. We render this offscreen tool and use it on the canvas as a whole.

Getting ready

You need to have cleared the recipes in *Chapter 5, Graphics – Canvas and Instructions*, to understand this recipe because you need to be able to differentiate between the Framebuffer and the canvas.

How to do it...

To complete this recipe, we will use just one Python file that has four rectangles with a texture that we are going to create in the Framebuffer. Follow these steps:

1. In the Python file, import the usual Kivy packages.
2. Also import the `Fbo` package.
3. Define the `MyW` class.
4. Define the `__init()__` method for the class.
5. Provide `canvas` in the method.
6. Create the `fbo` context.
7. Define four rectangles using the `fbo` texture.
8. Define the `fbo` context.
9. Then, define two rectangles of different colors:

```
import kivy
kivy.require('1.9.0') # Code tested in this version!
from kivy.app import App
from kivy.uix.widget import Widget
from kivy.graphics import Fbo, Color, Rectangle

classMyW(Widget):
    def __init__(self, **kwargs):
        super(MyW, self).__init__(**kwargs)

        withself.canvas:

            self.fbo = Fbo(size=(256, 256))

            Rectangle(size=(32, 32),
            texture=self.fbo.texture)
            Rectangle(pos=(32, 0), size=(64, 64),
            texture=self.fbo.texture)
            Rectangle(pos=(96, 0), size=(128, 128),
            texture=self.fbo.texture)
```

```
                    Rectangle(pos=(224, 0), size=(256, 128),
                    texture=self.fbo.texture)

            withself.fbo:
                Color(1, 0, 0, .8)
                Rectangle(size=(256, 64))
                Color(0, 1, 1, .8)
                Rectangle(size=(64, 256))

        class e7App(App):

            def build(self):
                return MyW()

        if __name__ == '__main__':
            e7App().run()
```

How it works...

In the __init__() method, we provide canvas to the app. We have the following line:

```
self.fbo = Fbo(size=(256, 256))
```

This has made the links between the canvas and Fbo. Also, it defins the size of the fbo screen. The next line is:

```
Rectangle(size=(32, 32), texture=self.fbo.texture)
```

This creates a rectangle with the texture taken from fbo and makes sure that the next three lines are equal. We have the following lines:

```
withself.fbo:
    Color(1, 0, 0, .8)
    Rectangle(size=(256, 64))
    Color(0, 1, 1, .8)
    Rectangle(size=(64, 256))
```

This draws what will be in fbo, and we use it as a texture in the canvas.

Optimizing graphics

Kivy is recommended because it makes a lot of optimizations by itself. Indeed, this permits the programmer who does not know how to use graphics and OpenGL to create applications with great graphical performance. However, you can always improve it using OpenGL code directly in Kivy, and besides the renderings presented in this chapter with the shaders, we have two additional considerations.

Getting ready

You need to have clear concepts of OpenGL to go deeper in this recipe, so it is useful to refer to the Kronos documentation at `https://www.khronos.org/opengles/sdk/docs/man/`.

How to do it...

In this recipe, we are going to review three examples to improve our graphics:

1. First, if we want to work with OpenGL directly in Kivy, we import it in the Python file of our app:

   ```
   from kivy.graphics.opengl import *
   ```

2. Here, we import all the OpenGL available methods. Now we can start to work with OpenGL instructions:

   ```
   glEnable(GL_DEPTH_TEST)
   ```

3. Next, we add our graphics and then we end the instructions with:

   ```
   glDisable(GL_DEPTH_TEST)
   ```

4. Directly in Kivy, while drawing in the canvas, optimize the graphics and do not repeat the colors unnecessarily. For example, if you have:

   ```
   <MyW1>:
       canvas:
           Color:
               rgb: 0,0,1
            Ellipse:
           pos: 0,0
           size: 50,50
           Color:
               rgb: 1,0,1
       Rectangle:
           pos: 100,0
           size: 50,50
           Color:
               rgb: 0,0,1
       Triangle:
               points: 200,0,250,50,250,0
   ```

   It is much better to arrange them as:

   ```
   <MyW1>:
       canvas:
           Color:
               rgb: 0,0,1
   ```

```
Ellipse:
    pos: 0,0
    size: 50,50
Triangle:
    points: 200,0,250,50,250,0
    Color:
        rgb: 1,0,1
Rectangle:
    pos: 100,0
    size: 50,50
```

5. Note how in the second case we arranged `Ellipse` and `Triangle` one after the other to use just one color instruction because they are of the same color.

6. The second consideration is to do with `Fbo`. You clean `Fbo` before reusing it, with the instructions:

```
self.fbo = Fbo(size=self.size)
withself.fbo:
ClearColor(0, 0, 0, 0)
ClearBuffers()
```

This is important because any other way to clean it is not useful.

There's more...

Actually, not all OpenGL standards are already implemented in Kivy, so we need to be careful with it. Some of the most important standards that are not implemented are:

▸ `glGetShaderPrecisionFormat()`

▸ `glGetVertexAttribPointerv()`

▸ `glReleaseShaderCompiler()`

▸ `glShaderBinary()`

See also

If you want to go deeper into graphics, you should read the OpenGL documentation for Kivy at `http://kivy.org/docs/api-kivy.graphics.opengl.html` and the Khronos site.

7
The API in Detail

In this chapter, we will cover the following:

- ▶ Getting to know the API
- ▶ Using the asynchronous data loader
- ▶ Logging objects
- ▶ Parsing
- ▶ Applying utils
- ▶ Leveraging the factory object
- ▶ Working with audio
- ▶ Working with the video
- ▶ Working with a camera
- ▶ Using spelling
- ▶ Adding effects
- ▶ Advanced text manipulation

Introduction

Kivy is actually an API for Python, which lets us create cross-platform apps. An **application programming interface** (**API**) is a set of routines, protocols, and tools to build software applications. Generally, we call Kivy as a framework because it also has procedures and instructions, such as the Kv language, which are not present in Python. Frameworks are environments that come with support programs, compilers, code libraries, tool sets, and APIs.

In this chapter, we want to review the Kivy API reference. We will go through some useful classes of the API. Every time we import a Kivy package, we will be dealing with an API. Even though the usual imports are from `kivy.uix`, there are more options and classes in the Kivy API. The Kivy developers have created the API reference, which you can refer to online at `http://kivy.org/docs/api-kivy.html` for an exhaustive information.

Getting to know the API

Our starting point is going to be the `App` class, which is the base to create Kivy applications. In this recipe, we are going to create a simple app that uses some resources from this class.

Getting ready

Please go through the *Building your Interfaces* recipe from *Chapter 1, Kivy and the Kv Language*, which is important and will help you see the role of the `App` class in the code.

How to do it...

To complete this recipe, we will create a Python file to make the resources present in the `App` class. Let's follow these steps:

1. Import the `kivy` package.
2. Import the `App` package.
3. Import the `Widget` package.
4. Define the `MyW()` class.
5. Define the `e1App()` class instanced as `App`.
6. Define the `build()` method and give an icon and a title to the app.
7. Define the `on_start()` method.
8. Define the `on_pause()` method.
9. Define the `on_resume()` method.
10. Define the `on_stop()` method.
11. End the app with the usual lines:

```
import kivy
from kivy.app import App
from kivy.uix.widget import Widget

class MyW(Widget):
    pass
```

```
class e1App(App):

    def build(self):
        self.title = 'My Title'
        self.icon = 'f0.png'
        returnMyW()

    def on_start(self):
        print("Hi")
        return True

    def on_pause(self):
        print("paused")
        return True

    def on_resume(self):
        print("active")
        pass

    def on_stop(self):
        print("Bye!")
        pass

if __name__ == '__main__':
    e1App().run()
```

How it works...

In the second line, we import the most common `kivy` package. This is the most used element of the API because it permits to create applications. The third line is an importation from `kivy.uix` that could be the second most used element, because the majority of the widgets are in there.

In the `e1app` class, we have the usual `build()` method where we have the line:

```
self.title = 'My Title'
```

We are providing a title to the app. As you can remember, the default title should be `e1` because of the class's name, but now we are using the title that we want. We have the next line:

```
self.icon = 'f0.png'
```

We are giving the app an icon. The default is the Kivy logo, but with this instruction, we are using the image in the file `f0.png`. In addition, we have the following method:

```
def on_start(self):
    print("Hi")
    return True
```

It is in charge of all actions performed when the app starts. In this case, it will print the word **Hi** in the console. The method is as follows:

```
def on_pause(self):
    print("paused")
    return True
```

This is the method that is performed when the app is paused when it is taken off from RAM. This event is very common when the app is running in a mobile device. You should return *True* if your app can go into pause mode, otherwise return *False* and your application will be stopped. In this case, we will print the word **paused** in the console, but it is very important that you save important information in the long-term memory, because there can be errors in the resume of the app and most mobiles don't allow real multitasking and pause apps when switching between them. This method is used with:

```
def on_resume(self):
    print("active")
    pass
```

The `on_resume` method is where we verify and correct any error in the sensible data of the app. In this case, we are only printing the word **active** in the console. The last method is:

```
def on_stop(self):
    print("Bye!")
    pass
```

It is where all the actions are performed before the app closes. Normally, we save data and take statistics in this method, but in this recipe, we just say **Bye!** in the console.

There's more...

There is another method, the `load_kv` method, that you can invoke in the `build` method, which permits to make our own selection of the KV file to use and not the default one. You only have to add follow line in the `build()` method:

```
self.load_kv(filename='e2.kv')
```

The natural way to go deeper in this recipe is to take a look at the special characteristics that the App has for the multiplatform support that Kivy provides. This is exactly what we want to cover in *Chapter 8, Packaging our Apps for PC* and *Chapter 9, Kivy for Mobile Devices*.

Using the asynchronous data loader

An asynchronous data loader permits to load images even if its data is not available. It has diverse applications, but the most common is to load images from the Internet, because this makes our app always useful even in the absence of Web connectivity. In this recipe, we will generate an app that loads an image from the Internet.

Getting ready

We did a similar image loading in the *Creating and Using Atlas* recipe of the *Chapter 6, Advanced Graphics – Shaders and Rendering*. So, you should see difference between the two loads.

We need an image from the Web, so find it and grab its URL.

How to do it...

We need only a Python file and the URL in this recipe. To complete the recipe:

1. Import the usual `kivy` package.
2. Import the `Image` and `Loader` packages.
3. Import the `Widget` package.
4. Define the `e2App` class.
5. Define the `_image_Loaded()` method, which loads the image in the app.
6. Define the `build()` method.
7. In this method, load the image in a proxy image.
8. Define the image variable instanced as `Image()`.
9. Return the image variable to display the load image:

```
import kivy
kivy.require('1.9.0')

from kivy.app import App
from kivy.uix.image import Image
```

```
from kivy.loader import Loader

class e2App(App):

    def _image_loaded(self, proxyImage):
        if proxyImage.image.texture:
            self.image.texture = proxyImage.image.texture

    def build(self):
        proxyImage = Loader.image(
        'http://iftucr.org/IFT/ANL_files/artistica.jpg')
        proxyImage.bind(on_load=self._image_loaded)
        self.image = Image()
        return self.image

if __name__ == '__main__':
    e2App().run()
```

How it works...

The line that loads the image is:

```
proxyImage = Loader.image(
'http://iftucr.org/IFT/ANL_files/artistica.jpg')
```

We assign the image to the `proxyImage` variable because we are not sure if the image exists or could be retrieved from the Web. We have the following line:

```
proxyImage.bind(on_load=self._image_loaded)
```

We bind the event `on_load` to the variable `proxyImage`. The used method is:

```
def _image_loaded(self, proxyImage):
    if proxyImageifproxyImage.image.texture:
    self.image.texture =      proxyImage.image.texture
```

It verifies whether the image is loaded or not; if not, then it does not change the image. This is why, we said that this will load in an asynchronous way.

There's more...

You can also load an image from a file in the traditional way. We have the following line:

```
proxyImage = Loader.image(
'http://iftucr.org/IFT/ANL_files/artistica.jpg')
```

Replace the preceding line with:

```
proxyImage = Loader.image('f0.png')
```

Here, `f0.png` is the name of the file to load.

Logging objects

The log in any software is useful for many aspects, one of them being exception handling. Kivy is always logging information about its performance. It creates a log file of every running of our app. Every programmer knows how helpful logging is for software engineering. In this recipe, we want to show information of our app in that log.

How to do it...

We will use a Python file with the `MyW()` usual class where we will raise an error and display it in the Kivy log. To complete the recipe, follow these steps:

1. Import the usual `kivy` package.
2. Import the `Logger` packages.
3. Define the `MyW()` class.
4. Trigger an info log.
5. Trigger a debug log.
6. Perform an exception.
7. Trigger an exception log:

```
import kivy
kivy.require('1.9.0')
from kivy.app import App
from kivy.uix.widget import Widget
from kivy.logger import Logger

class MyW(Widget):
    Logger.info('MyW: This is an info message.')
    Logger.debug('MyW: This is a debug message.')
    try:
        raise Exception('exception')
    except Exception:
```

```
            Logger.exception('Something happened!')
class e3App(App):

    def build(self):
        return MyW()

if __name__ == '__main__':
    e3App().run()
```

How it works...

In this recipe, we are creating three logs. The first in the line is:

> `Logger.info('MyW: This is an info message.')`

This is an info log, which is associated just with the supplementary information. The label `MyW` is just a convention, but you could use it in whatever way you like. Using the convention, we track where the log was performed in the code. We will see a log made by that line as:

`[INFO            ] [MyW        ] This is an info message.`

The next line also performs a log notation:

> `Logger.debug('MyW: This is a debug message.')`

This line will produce a debug log commonly used to debug the code. Consider the following line:

> `Logger.exception('Something happened!')`

This will perform an error log, which would look like:

`[ERROR           ] Something happened!`

In addition to the three present in this recipe, you can use trace, warning, and critical logging objects.

There's more...

We also have the trace, warning, error, and critical methods in the `Logger` class that work similarly to the methods described in this recipe.

The log file by default is located in the `.kivy/logs/` folder of the user running the app, but you can always change it in the Kivy configuration file.

Additionally, you can access the last 100 messages for debugging purposes even if the logger is not enabled. This is made with the help of `LoggerHistory` as follows:

```
from kivy.logger import LoggerHistory
print(LoggerHistory.history)
```

So, the console will display the last 100 logs.

See also

More information about logging can be found at
`http://kivy.org/docs/api-kivy.logger.html`.

Parsing

Actually, Kivy has the parser package that helps in the CSS parsing. Even though it is not a complete parsing, it helps to parse instructions related to a framework. The recipe will show some that you could find useful in your context.

How to do it...

The parser package has eight classes, so we will work in Python to review all of them. Let's follow the next steps:

1. Import the `parser` package.

   ```
   from kivy.parser import *
   ```

2. Parse a color from a string.

   ```
   parse_color('#090909')
   ```

3. Parse a string to a string.

   ```
   parse_string("(a,1,2)")a
   ```

4. Parse a string to a boolean value.

   ```
   parse_bool("0")
   ```

5. Parse a string to a list of two integers.

   ```
   parse_int2("12 54")
   ```

6. Parse a string to a list of four floats.

   ```
   parse_float4('54 87.13 35 0.9')
   ```

7. Parse a file name.

   ```
   parse_filename('e7.py')
   ```

Finally, we have `parse_int` and `parse_float`, which are aliases of int and float, respectively.

How it works...

In the second step, we parse any of the common ways to define a color (that is, RGB(r, g, b), RGBA(r, g, b, a), aaa, rrggbb, #aaa or #rrggbb) to a Kivy color definition.

The third step takes off the single or double quotes of the string. The fourth step takes a string True for 1 and False for 0 and parses it to its respective boolean value.

The last step is probably very useful because it permits verification if that file name is a file available to be used. If the file is found, the resource path is returned.

See also

To use a more general parser, you can use ply package for Python. Visit `https://pypi.python.org/pypi/ply` for further information.

Applying utils

There are some methods in Kivy that cannot be arranged in any other class. They are miscellaneous and could be helpful in some contexts. In this recipe, we will see how to use them.

How to do it...

In the spirit to show all the methods available, let's work directly in Python. To do the package tour, follow these steps:

1. Import the `kivy` package.

```
from kivy.utils import *
```

2. Find the intersection between two lists.

```
intersection(('a',1,2), (1,2))
```

3. Find the difference between two lists.

```
difference(('a',1,2), (1,2))
```

4. Convert a tuple in a string.

```
strtotuple("1,2")
```

5. Transform a hex string color to a Kivy color.

    ```
    get_color_from_hex('#000000')
    ```

6. Transform a Kivy color to a hex value.

    ```
    get_hex_from_color((0, 1, 0))
    ```

7. Get a random color.

    ```
    get_random_color(alpha='random')
    ```

8. Evaluate if a color is transparent.

    ```
    is_color_transparent((0,0,0,0))
    ```

9. Limit the value between a minimum value and maximum value.

    ```
    boundary(a,1,2)
    ```

10. Interpolate between two values.

    ```
    interpolate(10, 50, step=10)
    ```

11. Mark a function as deprecated.

    ```
    deprecated(MyW)
    ```

12. Get the platform where the app is running.

    ```
    platform()
    ```

How it works...

Almost every method presented in this recipe has a transparent syntax. Let's get some detail on two of the steps. The ninth step is the boundary method. It evaluates the value of a, and if this is between 1 and 2, it conserves its value; if it is lower than 1, the method returns 1; if it is greater than 2, the method returns 2.

The eleventh step is associated with the warning by using the function MyW; when this function is called the first time, the warning will be triggered.

See also

If you want to explore this package in detail, you can visit http://kivy.org/docs/api-kivy.utils.html.

Leveraging the factory object

The factory object represents the last step to create our own widgets because the factory can be used to automatically register any class or module and instantiate classes from any place in the app. This is a Kivy implementation of the factory pattern where a factory is an object to create other objects. This also opens a lot of possibilities to create dynamic codes in Kivy. In this recipe, we will register one of our widgets.

Getting ready

We will use an adaptation of the code in the recipe *Creating Widgets* of *Chapter 6, Advanced Graphics – Shaders and Rendering* to register the widget as a factory object. Copy the file in the same location of this recipe with the name e7.py.

How to do it...

In this recipe, we will use one of our simple Python files where we will register our widget using the factory package. Follow these steps:

1. Import the usual `kivy` packages.

2. In addition, import the `Factory` package.

3. Register the `MyWidget` object from the file of the *Chapter 6, Advanced Graphics – Shaders and Rendering*.

4. In the `build()` method of the usual `e8App`, return `Factory.MyWidget`.

```
import kivy
kivy.require('1.9.0')

from kivy.app import App
from kivy.uix.widget import Widget
from kivy.factory import Factory

Factory.register('MyWidget', module='e7')

classMyW(Widget):
    pass

class e8App(App):

    def build(self):
        returnFactory.MyWidget()

if __name__ == '__main__':
    e8App().run()
```

How it works...

Let us note how the magic is done in the following line:

```
Factory.register('MyWidget', module='e7')
```

This line creates the factory object named `MyWidget` and let's use it as we want. See how `e7` is the name of the file that we have brought from the recipe of the *Chapter 6, Advanced Graphics – Shaders and Rendering*. Actually, this sentence also will create a file named `e7.pyc`, which we can use as a replacement of the file `e7.py` if want to distribute our code; now it is not necessary to give the `e7.py`, since just the `e7.pyc` file is enough.

There's more...

This registration is actually permanent, so if you wish to change the registration in the same code, you need to unregister the object. For example, see the following:

```
Factory.unregister('MyWidget')
Factory.register('MyWidget', cls=CustomWidget)
New_widget = Factory.MyWidget()
```

See also

If you want to know more about this amazing package, you can visit `http://kivy.org/docs/api-kivy.factory.html`.

Working with audio

Nowadays, the audio integration in our app is vital. You could not realize a video game without audio or an app that does not use multimedia. We will create a sample with just one button which when pressed plays an audio.

Getting ready

We need an audio file in this recipe in the traditional audio formats (mp3, mp4, wav, wma, b-mtp, ogg, spx, midi). If you do not have any, you always can get one from sites such as `https://www.freesound.org`.

How to do it...

We will use a simple Python file with just one widget to play the audio file. To complete the recipe, let's follow these steps:

1. Import the usual `kivy` package.

2. Import the `SoundLoader` package.

3. Define the `MyW()` class.

4. Define the `__init__()` method.

5. Create a button with the label `Play`.

6. Bind the press action with the `press()` method.

7. Add the widget to the app.

8. Define the `press()` method.

9. Call the `SoundLoader.sound()` method for your audio file.

10. Play it with the `play()` method:

```python
import kivy
kivy.require('1.9.0')

from kivy.app import App
from kivy.uix.widget import Widget
from kivy.uix.button import Button
from kivy.core.audio import SoundLoader

class MyW(Widget):

    def __init__(self, **kwargs):
        super(MyW, self).__init__(**kwargs)
        b1=Button(text='Play')
        b1.bind(on_press=self.press)
        self.add_widget(b1)

    def press(self, instance):
        sound = SoundLoader.load('owl.wav')
        if sound:
            print("Sound found at %s" % sound.source)
            print("Sound is %.3f seconds" % sound.length)
            sound.play()
            print('playing')
```

```
class e4App(App):

    def build(self):
        returnMyW()

if __name__ == '__main__':
    e4App().run()
```

How it works...

In this recipe, the audio file is a load in the line:

```
sound = SoundLoader.load('owl.wav')
```

Here, we use a `.wav` format. Look at the following line:

```
if sound:
```

We handle that the file has been correctly loaded. We have the next line:

```
print("Sound found at %s" % sound.source)
```

This prints the name of the file that has been loaded in the console. The next line prints the duration of the file in seconds. See the other line:

```
sound.play()
```

It is where the file is played in the app.

There's more...

Also, you can use the `seek()` and `stop()` methods to navigate to the audio file. Let's say that you want to play the audio after the first minute, you will use:

```
Sound.seek(60)
```

The parameter received by the `seek()` method must be in seconds.

See also

If you need more control of the audio, you should visit
`http://kivy.org/docs/api-kivy.core.audio.html`.

Working with video

The video reproduction is a useful tool for any app. In this app, we will load a widget to reproduce a video file in our app.

Getting ready

It is necessary to have a video file in the usual format to be reproduced in our app (`.avi`, `.mov`, `.mpg`, `.mp4`, `.flv`, `.wmv`, `.ogg`). If you do not have one, you can visit `https://commons.wikimedia.org/wiki/Main_Page` to get free media.

How to do it...

In this recipe, we are going to use a simple Python file to create our app within a player widget. To complete the task, follow these:

1. Import the usual `kivy` packages.
2. Import the `VideoPlayer` package.
3. Define the `MyW()` class.
4. Define the `__init__()` method.
5. Define `videoplayer` with your video.
6. Add the video player to the app.

```python
import kivy
kivy.require('1.9.0')
from kivy.app import App
from kivy.uix.widget import Widget
from kivy.uix.videoplayer import VideoPlayer

class MyW(Widget):

    def __init__(self, **kwargs):
        super(MyW, self).__init__(**kwargs)
        player= VideoPlayer(
        source='GOR.MOV',state='play',
        options={'allow_stretch': True},
        size=(600,600))
        self.add_widget(player)

class e5App(App):
```

```
        def build(self):
            returnMyW()

    if __name__ == '__main__':
        e5App().run()
```

How it works...

In this recipe, the most important line is:

```
player= VideoPlayer(
source='GOR.MOV',state='play',
options={'allow_stretch': True},
size=(600,600))
```

This line loads the file, sets some options, and gives the size to the widget. The option `'allow stretch'` let's you modify the image of the video or not. In our recipe, `'allow stretch'` is permitted, so the images will be maximized to fit in the widget.

There's more...

You can also integrate subtitles or annotations to the video in an easy way. You only need a JSON-based file with the same name as the video, in the same location with `.jsa` extension. For example, let's use this content in the `.jsa` file:

```
[
{"start": 0, "duration": 2,
"text": "Here your text"},
{"start": 2, "duration": 2, "bgcolor": [0.5, 0.2, 0.4, 0.5],
"text": "You can change the background color"}
]
```

The `"start"` sentence locates in which second the annotation will show up in the video and the `"duration"` sentence gives the time in seconds that the annotation will be in the video.

See also

There are some apps that need more control of the video, so you can visit `http://kivy.org/docs/api-kivy.core.video.html` for better understanding.

Working with a camera

It is very common that almost all our personal devices have a camera. So you could find thousands of ways to use a camera signal in your app. In this recipe, we want to create an app that takes control of the camera present in a device.

Getting ready

Actually, you need to have the correct installation of the packages that permits you to interact with a camera. You can review `http://kivy.org/docs/faq.html#gstreamer-compatibility` to check if your installation is suitable.

How to do it...

We are going to use the Python and KV files in this recipe. The KV file will deal with the camera and button to interact with it. The Python code is one of our usual Python files with the definition of the root widget. Let's follow these steps:

1. In the KV file, define the `<MyW>` rule.

2. In the rule, define `BoxLayout` with a vertical orientation.

3. Inside the `Layout`, define the camera widget with play property as `false`.

4. Also, define the `ToggleButton` with the press property swifts between play and not play:

```
<MyW>:
    BoxLayout:
        orientation: 'vertical'
        Camera:
            id: camera
            play: False
        ToggleButton:
            text: 'Play'
            on_press: camera.play = not camera.play
            size_hint_y: None
            height: '48dp'
```

5. In the Python file, import the usual packages.

6. Define the `MyW()` class instanced as `BoxLayout`:

```
import kivy
kivy.require('1.9.0')
from kivy.app import App
```

```
from kivy.uix.widget import Widget
from kivy.uix.boxlayout import BoxLayout

class MyW(BoxLayout):
    pass

class e6App(App):
    def build(self):
        return MyW()

if __name__ == '__main__':
    e6App().run()
```

There's more...

If we have a device with more than one camera, for example, the handheld device front and rear camera, you can use the index property to switch between them. We have the following line:

id: camera

Add this line in the KV file:

index: 0

The preceding line is to select the first camera, index:1 for the second, and so on.

Using spelling

Depending on the kind of app that we will develop, we will need to spellcheck text provided by the user. In the Kivy API, there is a package to deal with it. In this recipe, we will give an example of how to do it.

Getting ready

If you are not using Mac OS X (or OS X as Apple called now), we will need to install the Python package: **PyEnchant**. For the installation, let's use the pip tool as follows:

pip install PyEnchant

How to do it...

Because this recipe could use it in different contexts, let's work directly in Python. We want to make some suggestions to the word misspelled. To complete the task, follow these steps:

1. Import the `Spelling` package.

   ```
   from kivy.core.spelling import Spelling
   ```

2. Instance the object s as `Spelling()`.

   ```
   s = Spelling()
   ```

3. List the available language.

   ```
   s.list_languages()
   ```

4. In this case, select U.S. English.

   ```
   s.select_language('en_US')
   ```

5. Ask for a suggestion to the object s.

   ```
   s.suggest('mispell')
   ```

How it works...

The first four steps actually set the kind of suggestion that we want. The fifth step makes the suggestion in line:

```
s.suggest('mispell')
```

The output of the expression is:

[u'misspell', u'ispell']

The output is in the order of the used frequency, so misspell is the most probable word that the user wanted to use.

Adding effects

Effects are one of the most important advances in the computer graphics field. The physics engines help create better effects, and they are under continuous improvement. Effects are pleasing to the end user. They change the whole experience.

The kinetic effect is the mechanism that Kivy uses to approach this technology. This effect can be used in diverse applications from the movement of a button to the simulation of real graphical environments. In this recipe, we will review how to set the effect to use it in our apps.

Getting ready

We are going to use some concepts from physics in this recipe, so it's necessary to have the clear basics.

 You should start reading about this on Wikipedia at `http://en.wikipedia.org/wiki/Acceleration`.

How to do it...

As the applications of this effect are as creative as you want, we are going to work directly in Python to set up the effect. Let's follow these steps:

1. Import the `KineticEffect` package.

    ```
    from kivy.effects.kinetic import KineticEffect
    ```

2. Instance the object effect as `KineticEffect()`.

    ```
    effect = KineticEffect()
    ```

3. Start the effect at second `10`.

    ```
    effect.start(10)
    ```

4. Update the effect at second `15`.

    ```
    effect.update(15)
    ```

5. Update the effect again at second `30`.

    ```
    effect.update(30)
    ```

6. You can always add friction to the movement.

    ```
    effect.friction
    ```

7. You can also update the velocity.

    ```
    effect.update_velocity(30)
    ```

8. Stop the effect at second `48`.

    ```
    effect.stop(48)
    ```

9. Get the final velocity.

    ```
    effect.velocity()
    ```

10. Get the value in seconds.

    ```
    effect.value()
    ```

How it works...

What we are looking for in this recipe is step 9:

```
effect.velocity()
```

The final velocity is how we can use to describe the movement of any object in a realistic way. As the distances are relatively fixed in the app, you need the velocity to describe any motion. We could incrementally repeat the steps to vary the velocity.

There's more...

There are other three effects based on the Kinetic effect, which are:

- ▶ **ScrollEffect**: This is the base class used to implement an effect. It only calculates scrolling and overscroll.
- ▶ **DampedScrollEffect**: This uses the overscroll information to allow the user to drag more than is expected. Once the user stops the drag, the position is returned to one of the bounds.
- ▶ **OpacityScrollEffect**: This uses the overscroll information to reduce the opacity of the ScrollView widget. When the user stops the drag, the opacity is set back to 1.

See also

If you want to go deeper in this topic, you should visit:
http://kivy.org/docs/api-kivy.effects.html.

Advanced text manipulation

Text is one of the most commonly used contents used in the apps. The recipe will create an app with a label widget where we will use text rendering to make our **Hello World**.

How to do it...

We are going to use one simple Python files that will just show our **Hello World** text. To complete the recipe:

1. Import the usual kivy packages.
2. Also, import the label package.
3. Define the e9app class instanced as app.
4. Define the method build() to the class.

5. Return the label widget with our `Hello World` text.

```
import kivy
kivy.require('1.9.0') # Code tested in this version!
from kivy.app import App
from kivy.uix.label import Label

class e9App(App):

    def build(self):
        return Label(text='Hello
        [ref=world][color=0000ff]World[/color][/ref]',
        markup=True, font_size=80, font_name='DroidSans')

if __name__ == '__main__':
    e9App().run()
```

How it works...

Here is the line:

```
return Label(text='Hello
[ref=world][color=0000ff]World[/color][/ref]', markup=True,
font_size=80, font_name='DroidSans')
```

This is the place where the rendering is done. Look at the text parameter where the token `[ref]` permits us to reference that specific part of the text (for example, to detect a click in the word `World`) the token `[color]` gives a particular color to that part of the text. The parameter `markup=True` allows the use of tokens. The parameters `font_size` and `font_name` will let you select the size and font to use for the text.

There's more...

There are others parameter with evident functions that the label widget can receive like:

- ▸ bold=*False*
- ▸ italic=*False*
- ▸ halign=*left*
- ▸ valign=*bottom*
- ▸ shorten=*False*
- ▸ text_size=*None*
- ▸ color=*None*
- ▸ line_height=*1.0*

Here, they have been evaluated with their default values.

See also

If you are interested in creating even more varieties of texts, you can visit `http://kivy.org/docs/api-kivy.uix.label.html#kivy.uix.label.Label` or `http://kivy.org/docs/api-kivy.core.text.html`.

8

Packaging our Apps for PC

In this chapter, we will cover the following:

- ▶ Packaging for Windows
- ▶ Including multimedia for Windows
- ▶ Running apps in Windows
- ▶ Packaging for Mac OS
- ▶ Including multimedia for Mac OS
- ▶ Running apps in Mac OS
- ▶ Packaging for Linux
- ▶ Including multimedia for Linux
- ▶ Running apps in Linux

Introduction

This chapter represents the final step that any app needs to follow before being distributed. Probably, this step is the most valuable Kivy characteristic because if we want to distribute our app to any platform, we do not need to change any piece of our app code. In this chapter, we will show the mentioned characteristic using the same code and packaging it for the three majorly used platforms.

We will also review how to package our app so that it can be distributed in an insolated way without the need of installing Kivy or Python. This practice is very common in Python using PyInstaller, but we are going to tweak it to use Kivy as well. We need to have installed the specific platform in which you want your app to be packaged, and the reason is that PyInstaller should incorporate the Kivy distribution in the package for the target platform.

Packaging for Windows

Nowadays, Microsoft Windows remains one of the most used operating systems in the world. So, it is convenient to have the possibility of distributing our apps to these users. In this recipe, we will make a package of one complex app that uses three files. This package will be a single file that can run without installing Kivy or Python on a Windows machine.

Getting ready

First, you need a machine or a virtual machine running Microsoft Windows with the Kivy portable version installed. You can check the recipe *Installing Kivy* in *Chapter 1, Kivy and the Kv Language*. Also, you need to install the PyInstaller package. There are several methods to do this, but, for our purpose, the best way is to download source files from `https://pypi.python.org/pypi/PyInstaller/2.1`.

Decompress the package in the directory of your preference. We will then be working in that directory.

In addition, if you are using Kivy 1.9.0, the portable package does not include Pygame libraries, so you should install them. You may download them from `http://www.pygame.org/download.shtml`.

Select the `pygame-1.9.2a0.win32-py2.7.msi` file, run it, and use your Kivy 1.9.0 portable package folder as an installation folder.

Of course, we will need an app to be packaged. Thus, we are going to use a very similar app to the one in the recipe *Leveraging factory* in *Chapter 7, The API in Detail*. However, we will add a KV file to provide a canvas to the app. First, let's see the KV file named `e1.kv`:

```
# e1.kv
<MyW>:
    canvas:
        Ellipse:
            pos: 0,0
            size: 50,50
        Rectangle:
            pos: 100,0
            size: 50,50
        Triangle:
            points: 200,0,250,50,250,0
        Line:
            points: 300,0,350,300
```

This is where we draw an ellipse, a rectangle, a triangle, and a line in the background of the app. Now, the file e0.py contains our custom widget:

```python
# e0.py
import kivy
kivy.require('1.9.0') # replace with your current kivy version !

from kivy.app import App
from kivy.uix.widget import Widget
from kivy.graphics import Color, Ellipse, Line
from kivy.factory import Factory

class MyWidget1(Widget):
    def on_touch_down(self, touch):
        with self.canvas:
            Color(1, 1, 0)
            d = 30.
            Ellipse(pos=(touch.x - d / 2, touch.y - d / 2),
            size=(d, d))
            touch.ud['line'] = Line(points=(touch.x, touch.y))

    def on_touch_move(self, touch):
        touch.ud['line'].points += [touch.x, touch.y]

Factory.register('MyWidget1', cls=MyWidget1)

class e0App(App):

    def build(self):
        return  Factory.MyWidget1()

if __name__ == '__main__':
    e0App().run()
```

Remember that we do not use this file directly, but we need the compiled version e0.pyc that is automatically generated when we call the e0.py file in the e1.py file:

```python
# e1.py
import kivy
kivy.require('1.9.0') # replace with your current kivy version !

from kivy.app import App
from kivy.uix.widget import Widget
```

```
from kivy.factory import Factory

Factory.register('MyWidget1', module='e0')

class MyW(Widget):
    def __init__(self, **kwargs):
        super(MyW, self).__init__(**kwargs)
        self.add_widget(Factory.MyWidget1())

class e1App(App):

    def build(self):
        return MyW()

if __name__ == '__main__':
    e1App().run()
```

Finally, it is important to have a specific location of this file in our computer because we need it to create the package.

How to do it...

Now, we will create our Windows package and use the previously described three files. We are going to work with the Windows Command Prompt (cmd.exe) directly. To complete this recipe, follow these instructions:

1. Run kivy.bat.

2. Locate the directory that has the e0.pyc, e1.kv, and e1.py files in the following way:

    C:\Users\Me\Documents\e1app

3. Go to the PyInstaller directory.

4. In the Prompt, create the folder and specification file for your package as follows:

    python ynstaller.py -- name e1
    "C:\Users\Me\Documents\e1app\e1.py"

5. Open the file e1\e1.spec in your favorite text editor, and you should see the following:

    ```
    # -*- mode: python -*-
    a = Analysis(['C:\\Users\\Me\\Documents\\e1app\\e1.py'],
    pathex=['C:\\Users\\Me\\Downloads\\PyInstaller-2.1\\e1'],
    hiddenimports=[],
    hookspath=None,
    runtime_hooks=None)
    pyz = PYZ(a.pure)
    ```

```
exe = EXE(pyz,
a.scripts,
exclude_binaries=True,
          name='e1.exe',
          debug=False,
          strip=None,
     upx=True,
          console=True )
coll = COLLECT(exe,
a.binaries,
a.zipfiles,
a.datas,
               strip=None,
     upx=True,
               name='e1')
```

6. Add the header to the file as follows:

```
from kivy.tools.packaging.pyinstaller_hooks import
install_hooks
install_hooks(globals())
```

7. Remove the following line:

```
hookspath=None,
```

8. After the line coll = COLLECT(exe, add the following:

```
Tree('C:\\Users\\Me\\Documents\\e1app\\'),
Tree([f for f in os.environ.get('KIVY_SDL2_PATH',
'').split(';') if 'bin' in f][0]),
```

Now, the code will look like this:

```
# -*- mode: python -*-
from kivy.tools.packaging.pyinstaller_hooks import install_hooks
install_hooks(globals())

a = Analysis(['C:\\Users\\Me\\Documents\\e1app\\e1.py'],
pathex=['C:\\Users\\Me\\Downloads\\PyInstaller-2.1\\e1'],
hiddenimports=[],
runtime_hooks=None)
pyz = PYZ(a.pure)
exe = EXE(pyz,
a.scripts,
exclude_binaries=True,
          name='e1.exe',
          debug=False,
```

```
                      strip=None,
                      upx=True,
                      console=True )
        coll = COLLECT(exe,
            Tree('C:\\Users\\Me\\Documents\\e1app\\'),
            Tree([f for f in os.environ.get('KIVY_SDL2_PATH',
            '').split(';') if 'bin' in f][0]),
        a.binaries,
        a.zipfiles,
        a.datas,
                      strip=None,
        upx=True,
                      name='e1')
```

9. Inside the PyInstaller folder, generate the package with the following:

    ```
    python PyInstaller.py e1\e1.spec
    ```

    This will generate the folder e1\dist\e1\, which has our app packaged.

How it works...

In step 4, we created the specification file with the instructions to make the package of our app:

```
python pyinstaller.py -- name e1
"C:\Users\Me\Documents\e1app\e1.py"
```

The name option serves to create the folder where our app in PyInstaller will be located and the full location of our app specifies the app that needs to be packaged. The quotation marks are important in Microsoft Windows as it helps the PyInstaller to understand the correct location. The sixth step is where the magic happens. In this step, we included Kivy framework in our app package. The seventh step is fundamental because it permits PyInstaller to know that there exist hooks which need to be performed: in our case, the Kivy hook. In the eighth step, we added all the files that we had created and were present in the app folder of our package,. Also, in this step, we added some necessary DLLs for the Kivy version 1.9.0 that now use SDL2. Finally, in the tenth step, we created the package to be distributed.

There's more...

In step 9, we can change the file indication console=True to console=False, which does not display the console when the app is running. This is useful because the end user actually is not interested in the internal functionality of Kivy and the app.

Another useful tweak to our package is in step 4 where we can use the option -F:

```
python pyinstaller.py -F -- name e1
"C:\Users\Me\Documents\e1app\e1.py"
```

Also, we need to change step 8; now the addition must be done after the line `exe = EXE(pyz`, instead the `coll = COLLECT(exe`, because the variable `coll` is not present after the use of the option -F. This will package all the files in one single .exe file that will be located in the `e1\dist\` folder. This is nice because you just have to distribute a single file.

See also

You will have to go through the PyInstaller manual for further information at `http://pythonhosted.org/PyInstaller/`.

Including multimedia for Windows

The GStreamer modules are not included by default in the previous recipe. In that sense, you could not load multimedia files in our app packaged for Windows. This is because the GStreamer is highly dependent on the operating system. To solve this, we must import the OS Python package. In this recipe, we are going to create a package of an app that can run a video.

Getting ready

We will use an app that has multimedia. This recipe is going to be similar to *Working with video* in *Chapter 7*, *The API in Detail*. In that recipe, we used just one Python file.

```
# e2.py
import kivy
kivy.require('1.9.0') # replace with your current kivy version !

from kivy.app import App
from kivy.uix.widget import Widget
from kivy.uix.videoplayer import VideoPlayer

class MyW(Widget):

    def __init__(self, **kwargs):
        super(MyW, self).__init__(**kwargs)
player = VideoPlayer(source='GOR.MOV', state='play', options={'allow_
stretch': True}, size=(600,600))
        self.add_widget(player)

class e2App(App):

    def build(self):
```

```
        return MyW()

if __name__ == '__main__':
    e2App().run()
```

This app needs the file GOR.mov, which is the video to be played. Also, it is highly recommended to read the previous recipe in which the packaging process is explained in detail.

How to do it...

In order to create the package with multimedia, we are going to work in the Windows Command Prompt directly in the PyInstaller directory. Let's follow these steps:

1. Run kivy.bat.

2. Locate the directory that has the files: e2.py and GOR.mov, something like:

   C:\Users\Me\Documents\e2app

3. Go to the PyInstaller directory.

4. Create the folder and specification file for your package:

   python pyinstaller.py -- name e2
   "C:\Users\Me\Documents\e2app\e2.py"

5. Open the file e2\e2.spec in your favorite text editor and you must see the following:

```
# -*- mode: python -*-
a = Analysis(['C:\\Users\\Me\\Documents\\e2app\\e2.py'],
pathex=['C:\\Users\\Me\\Downloads\\PyInstaller-2.1\\e2'],
hiddenimports=[],
hookspath=None,
runtime_hooks=None)
pyz = PYZ(a.pure)
exe = EXE(pyz,
a.scripts,
exclude_binaries=True,
          name='e2.exe',
          debug=False,
          strip=None,
     upx=True,
          console=True )
coll = COLLECT(exe,
     a.binaries,
     a.zipfiles,
     a.datas,
          strip=None,
     upx=True,
          name='e2')
```

6. Add the header to the file:

```
import os
from kivy.tools.packaging.pyinstaller_hooks import
install_hooks
import kivy.core.video

install_hooks(globals())
gst_plugin_path=
os.environ.get('GST_PLUGIN_PATH').split('lib')[0]
```

7. Remove the following line:

```
hookspath=None,
```

8. After `coll = COLLECT(exe`, add the following:

```
Tree('C:\\Users\\Me\\Documents\\e1app\\'),
Tree(gst_plugin_path),
Tree(os.path.join(gst_plugin_path, 'bin')),
Tree([f for f in os.environ.get('KIVY_SDL2_PATH',
'').split(';') if 'bin' in f][0]),
```

9. Now the file will look like this:

```
# -*- mode: python -*-
import os
from kivy.tools.packaging.pyinstaller_hooks import install_hooks
import kivy.core.video

install_hooks(globals())
gst_plugin_path= os.environ.get('GST_PLUGIN_PATH').split('lib')[0]

a = Analysis(['C:\\Users\\Me\\Documents\\e2app\\e2.py'],
pathex=['C:\\Users\\Me\\Downloads\\PyInstaller-2.1\\e2'],
hiddenimports=[],
runtime_hooks=None)
pyz = PYZ(a.pure)
exe = EXE(pyz,
    a.scripts,
    exclude_binaries=True,
        name='e2.exe',
        debug=False,
        strip=None,
        upx=True,
        console=True )
coll = COLLECT(exe,
    Tree('C:\\Users\\Me\\Documents\\e2app\\'),
```

```
Tree(gst_plugin_path),
      Tree(os.path.join(gst_plugin_path, 'bin')),
Tree([f for f in os.environ.get('KIVY_SDL2_PATH', '').split(';')
if 'bin' in f][0]),
a.binaries,
a.zipfiles,
a.datas,
            strip=None,
upx=True,
            name='e2')
```

10. Always generate the package in the PyInstaller folder with this:

    python pyinstaller.py e2\e2.spec

    This will generate the folder e2\dist\e2\, which has our app packaged.

How it works...

The difference between the previous and this recipe is the use of GStreamer. The sixth step is:

gst_plugin_path= os.environ.get('GST_PLUGIN_PATH').split('lib')[0]

This is where we located the GStreamer directory in our platform.The eighth step is where we included the GStreamer with the information obtained in the sixth step, in these instructions:

Tree(gst_plugin_path),
Tree(os.path.join(gst_plugin_path, 'bin')),

Actually, we included the GStreamer directory in the second instruction that is in the subdirectory bin. The tenth generated the app package.

There's more...

We can use a personalized icon for our app. In Microsoft Windows, we need an .ico file to be used as icon for our app. The easiest way to create the image from one of the usual formats is by visiting a site like:

http://iconverticons.com/online/

Now, add the .ico file just after the line:

name='e2.exe',

Add this instruction:

```
icon='c:\\Users\\Me\\Documents\\e2app\\e2app.ico',
```

Repeat the tenth step.

See also

Do not forget to review the PyInstaller manual for further information. Visit `http://pythonhosted.org/PyInstaller/`.

Running apps in Windows

Now, we want to review some concepts to run our app on a specific Microsoft Windows platform. We are going to take the app and run it in Windows.

Getting ready

We need an app to run. For this purpose, let's use the app from the last recipe. Also, it would be useful to read the recipe *Running your code* in *Chapter 1*, *Kivy and the Kv Language* to understand how we personalize the app for running Microsoft Windows.

How to do it...

We now want to know how to run our app from the Command Prompt and give the correct size. To make this possible, let's follow these steps:

1. Run `kivy.bat`.

2. Locate the directory that has the files, `e2.py` and `GOR.mov`, something like:

   `C:\Users\Me\Documents\e2app\`

3. Open the file `e2.py` in your favorite editor.

4. After imports lines, add the following lines:

   ```
   from kivy.core.window import Window
   Window.system_size=(600,500)
   ```

5. In the Prompt, run the app:

   `C:\Users\Me\Documents\e2app> python e2.py`

How it works...

In this recipe, we ran our app in Windows. The first step was to load the path in the Python version with the Kivy framework. The fourth step was where we gave the size of our app window with the instruction:

```
Window.system_size=(600,500)
```

We are using the usual vector definition (*x, y*), so the window will be 600 pixels in the horizontal and 500 in the vertical. For information, remember that the most popular Microsoft Windows resolution is *1280 x 800*. Now, we do not need to call the module size in step 5. Step 5 is where we ran the app. It opened the app window and showed the Kivy login in the Prompt.

See also

If you want to know more about the Windows package, visit `http://kivy.org/docs/api-kivy.core.window.html`, and for Microsoft Windows resolutions, visit `http://windows.microsoft.com/en-us/windows/getting-best-display-monitor#getting-best-display-monitor=windows-7`.

Packaging for Mac OS

Apple is selling PCs at an extraordinary rate. In fact, there are a huge number using Mac OS. So, we should have a great market to distribute our apps. In this recipe, we are going to make a package with a complex app that uses three files. This package will be a single file that can be run without installing Kivy or Python on the Mac.

Getting ready

First, you need to run OS X and should have installed the `Kivy.app` version. You can check the recipe *Installing Kivy* in *Chapter 1, Kivy and the Kv Language*. Also, you need to install the PyInstaller package. There are different ways to do this, but for our purpose, the best is to download the source from `https://pypi.python.org/pypi/PyInstaller/2.1`.

Decompress the package in the directory of your preference. We will be working in this directory.

Additionally, if you are using Kivy 1.9.0, the portable package does not include Pygame libraries, so you will have to install them yourself by using the following code in the Prompt:

```
$ kivy -m pip install pygame
```

Of course, we will need an app to be packaged. We are going to use the app presented in the recipe *Packaging for Windows* in this chapter. We have three files `e0.pyc`, `e1.kv`, and `e1.py`.

How to do it...

Now, we will create our OS X package and will use the previously described three files. We are going to work in the terminal. Let's follow these instructions:

1. Locate the directory that has the files: e0.pyc, e1.kv, and e1.py, something like:

    /Users/Me/Documents/e1app/

2. Go to the PyInstaller directory.

3. In the terminal, create the folder and specification file for your package as follows:

    ```
    $ Kivy pyinstaller.py --windowed --name e1
    /Users/Me/Documents/e1app/e1.py
    ```

4. Open the file e1/e1.spec in your favorite text editor and you should see the following:

    ```python
    # -*- mode: python -*-
    a = Analysis(['/Users/Me/Documents/e1app/e1.py'],
    pathex=['/Users/Me/Documents/PyInstaller-2.1/e1'],
    hiddenimports=[],
    hookspath=None,
    runtime_hooks=None)
    pyz = PYZ(a.pure)
    exe = EXE(pyz,
    a.scripts,
    exclude_binaries=True,
            name='e1',
            debug=False,
            strip=None,
            upx=True,
            console=False )
    coll = COLLECT(exe,
        a.binaries,
            a.zipfiles,
            a.datas,
            strip=None,
        upx=True,
            name='e1')
    app = BUNDLE(coll,
            name='e1.app',
            icon=None)
    ```

5. Add the header to the file:

    ```python
    from kivy.tools.packaging.pyinstaller_hooks import
    install_hooks
    install_hooks(globals())
    ```

6. Remove the following line:

   ```
   hookspath=None,
   ```

7. After the line `coll = COLLECT(exe`, add:

   ```
   Tree('/Users/Me/Documents/e1app/'),
   ```

8. Now the code will look like:

   ```python
   # -*- mode: python -*-
   from kivy.tools.packaging.pyinstaller_hooks import install_hooks
   install_hooks(globals())

   a = Analysis(['/Users/Me/Documents/e1app/e1.py'],
               pathex=['/Users/Me/Documents/PyInstaller-2.1/e1'],
               hiddenimports=[],
                   runtime_hooks=None)
   pyz = PYZ(a.pure)
   exe = EXE(pyz,
             a.scripts,
        exclude_binaries=True,
             name='e1',
             debug=False,
             strip=None,
             upx=True,
             console=False )
   coll = COLLECT(exe,
        Tree('/Users/Me/Documents/e1app/'),
             a.binaries,
             a.zipfiles,
             a.datas,
             strip=None,
             upx=True,
             name='e1')
   app = BUNDLE(coll,
             name='e1.app',
             icon=None)
   ```

9. Always in the PyInstaller folder, generate the package with:

   ```
   $ kivy pyinstaller.py e1/e1.spec
   ```

   This will generate the folder `e1/dist/` in which the file `e1.app` is located.

How it works...

The first part of the process is in step 3 wherein we created the specification file to make the package of our app with the instruction:

```
$ Kivy pyinstaller.py --windowed --name e1
/Users/Me/Documents/e1app/e1.py
```

The `windowed` option gave PyInstaller the order to create the app without using the console. The name option served to create the folder where our app in the PyInstaller would be located and the full location of our app specified the app to be packaged. The fifth step is where the magic happened. Here, we included the Kivy framework in our app package. The sixth step is fundamental, which tells PyInstaller that hooks can be present in the file – the Kivy hook in this case. The seventh step is where we added to our package all the files present in our app folder, all the files that we had created. Finally, the ninth step is where we created the package to be distributed, the `e1.app` file.

There's more...

Also, we can generate a `dmg` file for our app. The `dmg` file helps in installing our app in the OS X environment. Let's move to the `dist` folder:

```
$ cd e1/dist/
```

Now, in this location, call `hdiutil` to create the `dmg` file with the instruction:

```
$ hdiutil create ./e1.dmg -srcfolder e1.app -ov
```

See also

Do not forget to review the PyInstaller manual for further information at `http://pythonhosted.org/PyInstaller/`.

Including multimedia for Mac OS

The package used to load multimedia is not included in the previous recipe. So, we need to modify the previous recipe if we want to use the GStreamer. In this recipe, we are going to create a package of an app that loads a video.

Getting ready

We will use an app within multimedia. We are going to utilize the same code of the app used in the recipe *Including multimedia for Windows* in this chapter, that is, the code in `e2.py` file.

This app needs the file GOR.mov, which is the video that will be played. Also, it is highly recommended to read the previous recipe as the packaging process is explained in detail there.

How to do it...

Again, we are going to work directly in the terminal of the PyInstaller directory. We will create a package for an app that plays a video. To complete this recipe, follow these steps:

1. Locate the directory that has the files: e2.py and GOR.mov, something like:

   /Users/Me/Documents/e2app/

2. Go to the PyInstaller directory.

3. Create the folder and specification file for your package:

   ```
   $ Kivy pyinstaller.py --windowed --name e2
   /Users/Me/Documents/e1app/e2.py
   ```

4. Open the file e2/e2.spec in your favorite text editor and you will see the following:

   ```python
   # -*- mode: python -*-
   a = Analysis(['/Users/Me/Documents/e2app/e2.py'],
   pathex=['/Users/Me/Documents/PyInstaller-2.1/e2'],
   hiddenimports=[],
   hookspath=None,
   runtime_hooks=None)
   pyz = PYZ(a.pure)
   exe = EXE(pyz,
       a.scripts,
       exclude_binaries=True,
           name='e1',
           debug=False,
       strip=None,
           upx=True,
           console=False )
   coll = COLLECT(exe,
   a.binaries,
   a.zipfiles,
   a.datas,
   strip=None,
   upx=True,
               name='e2')
   app = BUNDLE(coll,
               name='e2.app',
               icon=None)
   ```

5. Add the header to file:

```
import os
from kivy.tools.packaging.pyinstaller_hooks import
install_hooks

install_hooks(globals())
gst_plugin_path = os.environ.get('GST_PLUGIN_PATH').split(':')[0]
```

6. Inform PyInstaller that hooks are present by removing the following line:

```
hookspath=None,
```

7. After the line `coll = COLLECT(exe,` add:

```
Tree('/Users/Me/Documents/e2app/'),
Tree(os.path.join(gst_plugin_path, '..')),
```

Now the file should look like:

```
# -*- mode: python -*-
import os
from kivy.tools.packaging.pyinstaller_hooks import install_hooks

install_hooks(globals())
gst_plugin_path = os.environ.get('GST_PLUGIN_PATH').split(':')[0]

a = Analysis(['/Users/Me/Documents/e2app/e2.py'],
pathex=['/Users/Me/Documents/PyInstaller-2.1/e2'],
hiddenimports=[],
runtime_hooks=None)
pyz = PYZ(a.pure)
exe = EXE(pyz,
a.scripts,
exclude_binaries=True,
          name='e1',
              debug=False,
              strip=None,
upx=True,
        console=False )
coll = COLLECT(exe,
    Tree('/Users/Me/Documents/e1app/'),
Tree(os.path.join(gst_plugin_path, '..')),
a.binaries,
a.zipfiles,
a.datas,
```

```
                strip=None,
        upx=True,
        name='e2')
        app = BUNDLE(coll,
                name='e2.app',
                icon=None)
```

8. Always generate the package in the PyInstaller folder with:

   $ kivy pyinstaller.py e2/e2.spec

   This will generate the folder e2/dist/, which has our app packaged file e2.app.

How it works...

The difference between the previous and this recipe is the procedure where we do not have to use GStreamer in the fifth step:

gst_plugin_path = os.environ.get('GST_PLUGIN_PATH').split(':')[0]

This instruction located the GStreamer directory in your machine to be included in the package that we were going to create. The seventh step is where we actually included the GStreamer with the instruction:

```
        Tree(os.path.join(gst_plugin_path, '..')),
```

The tenth step is used to generate the app package.

There's more...

We can use a personalized icon for our app. In OS X, we need a .icns file that can be used as an icon for our app. A simple way to create the file from our chosen image in one of the usual formats can be done using http://iconverticons.com/online/.

Now, add the .icns file just after the following line:

name='e2app.app',

Add the following instruction:

icon='/Users/Me/Documents/e1app/e1.icns'

Then, repeat the tenth step.

Running apps in Mac OS

Now, we want to review some concepts so that we can run our app on the specific OS X platform. We are going to take the app and run it on OS X.

Getting ready

We need an app that can be run. For this purpose, let's use the same app that we used in our previous recipe. Also, it would be useful to read the recipe *Running your code* in *Chapter 1, Kivy and the Kv Language* in order to understand how we personalize the running for Microsoft Windows.

How to do it...

We want to know how to run our app from the terminal and how to give it the correct size. To make this possible, let's follow these:

1. Locate the directory that has the files, `e2.py` and `GOR.mov`, something like:

    /Users/Me/Documents/e2app/

2. Open the file `e2.py` in your favorite editor.

3. After the import lines, add these lines:

    ```
    from kivy.core.window import Window
    Window.system_size=(600,500)
    ```

4. In the terminal, run the app:

    ```
    $ kivye2.py
    ```

How it works...

The third step is where we are stated the size of our app window with the following instruction:

```
Window.system_size=(600,500)
```

We used the usual vector definition (*x*, *y*), so the window will be 600 pixels in the horizontal and 500 in the vertical. For information, remember that the most popular OS X resolution is *1440 x 900*. Now, we don't need to call the module size in the fourth step. This is the step where we ran the app. This will open the app window and will show the Kivy log in the Prompt.

See also

If you want to know more about the package, visit `http://kivy.org/docs/api-kivy.core.window.html`, and `https://support.apple.com/kb/PH19043?locale=en_US` for OS X resolutions.

Packaging for Linux

Finally, let's learn how to generate packages for Linux. In this recipe, we are going to make a package with a complex app that uses three files. This package will be a single file that can run without installing Kivy or Python in Linux.

Getting ready

First, you need to run a Linux distro and install Kivy, but you will need the development version. You can check how to do this at `http://kivy.org/docs/installation/installation.html#installation-devel`.

Also, you need to install the PyInstaller package. There are different ways to do it, but for our purpose, the way best is to download from the source `https://pypi.python.org/pypi/PyInstaller/2.0`.

Decompress the package in the directory of your preference. Actually, we are going to work inside this directory. We are using the 2.0 version instead of the 2.1 version to avoid some known conflicts with the Linux version.

Of course, we will need an app to be packaged. We are going to use the app presented in the recipe *Packaging for Windows* in this chapter. We have three files: `e0.pyc`, `e1.kv`, and `e1.py`.

How to do it...

We are going to create our Linux package, for which we will use the three previously mentioned files. We will work from the terminal. To complete the recipe, follow these instructions:

1. Locate the directory that has the files: `e0.pyc`, `e1.kv`, and `e1.py`, something like:

   /home/Me/Documents/e1app/

2. Go to the PyInstaller directory.

3. In the terminal, create the folder and specification file for your package:

   ```
   $ python pyinstaller.py -F --name e1
   /home/Me/Documents/e1app/e1.py
   ```

4. Open the file `e1/e1.spec` in your favorite text editor and you should see the following:

```
# -*- mode: python -*-
a = Analysis(['/home/Me/Documents/e1app/e1.py'],
pathex=['/home/Me/Documents/PyInstaller-2.0/e1'],
hiddenimports=[],
hookspath=None,
runtime_hooks=None)
pyz = PYZ(a.pure)
exe = EXE(pyz,
a.scripts,
a.binaries,
a.zipfiles,
a.datas,
                    name='e1',
          debug=False,
strip=None,
upx=True,
console=False )
```

5. Add the header to the file:

```
from kivy.tools.packaging.pyinstaller_hooks import
install_hooks
install_hooks(globals())
```

6. Remove the following lines:

```
hookspath=None,
runtime_hooks=None
```

7. After the line exe= Exe(pyz, add the following:

```
Tree('/home/Me/Documents/e1app/'),
```

Now the code will look like:

```
# -*- mode: python -*-
from kivy.tools.packaging.pyinstaller_hooks import install_hooks
install_hooks(globals())

a = Analysis(['/home/Me/Documents/e1app/e1.py'],
pathex=['/home/Me/Documents/PyInstaller-2.0/e1'],
hiddenimports=[])
pyz = PYZ(a.pure)
exe = EXE(pyz,
Tree('/home/Me/Documents/e1app/'),
a.scripts,
a.binaries,
```

```
        a.zipfiles,
        a.datas,
        name='e1',
        debug=False,
        strip=None,
        upx=True,
        console=False )
```

8. Always generate the package in the PyInstaller folder with:

   ```
   $ python pyinstaller.py e1/e1.spec
   ```

   This will generate the folder `e1/dist/` where the file `e1` is. The `e1` file can now be distributed.

Including multimedia for Linux

Again, we need to include the GStreamer to play videos or sounds in our packaged app. In this recipe, we are taking a simple app that plays a video and generate package with it.

Getting ready

We will use an app within multimedia. We are going to utilize the same app that we used in the *Including multimedia for Windows* and *Including multimedia for Mac OS* recipes in this chapter. It uses the `e2.py` code. Also, do read those recipes for further information.

This app needs the file `GOR.mov` which is the video that needs to be played. Also, it is highly recommended to read the previous recipe as the packaging process is explained in depth there.

How to do it...

Again, we are going to work directly in the terminal in the PyInstaller directory. We will create a package for an app that plays a video. To complete this recipe, follow the next steps:

1. Locate the directory that has the files, e2.py and GOR.mov, something like:

   /home/Me/Documents/e2app/

2. Go to the PyInstaller directory.

3. Create the folder and specification file for your package:

   ```
   $ python pyinstaller.py -F --name e2
   /home/Me/Documents/e1app/e2.py
   ```

4. Open the file `e2/e2.spec` in your favorite text editor.

5. Add the header to the file:

```
import os
from kivy.tools.packaging.pyinstaller_hooks import
install_hooks

install_hooks(globals())
gst_plugin_path = os.environ.get('GST_PLUGIN_PATH').split(':')[0]
```

6. Remove these lines:

```
hookspath=None,
runtime_hooks=None
```

7. After the line `exe = EXE(pyz,`add:

```
Tree('/home/Me/Documents/e2app/'),
Tree(os.path.join(gst_plugin_path, '..')),
```

8. Now the file will look like:

```
# -*- mode: python -*-
import os
from kivy.tools.packaging.pyinstaller_hooks import install_hooks

install_hooks(globals())
gst_plugin_path = os.environ.get('GST_PLUGIN_PATH').split(':')[0]

a = Analysis(['/home/Me/Documents/e1app/e1.py'],
pathex=['/home/Me/Documents/PyInstaller-2.0/e1'],
hiddenimports=[])
pyz = PYZ(a.pure)
exe = EXE(pyz,
Tree('/home/Me/Documents/e2app/'),
Tree(os.path.join(gst_plugin_path, '..')),
a.scripts,
a.binaries,
a.zipfiles,
a.datas,
name='e1',
debug=False,
strip=None,
upx=True,
console=False )
```

9. Always generate the package in the PyInstaller folder with:

```
$ python pyinstaller.py e2/e2.spec
```

This will generate the folder `e2/dist/`, which has our app packaged file `e2`.

Running apps in Linux

This process should be used to run our app in the specific Linux distribution. We are going to take the app and run it in a proper way in our distribution.

Getting ready

We need an app to run. For this purpose, let's use the same app from the previous recipe. Also, it could be useful to read the recipe *Running your code* in *Chapter 1, Kivy and the Kv Language* in order to understand how we customize the running for Microsoft Windows. Also, if you want to see the differences between the different PC platforms, then go through *Running apps in Windows* and *Running apps in Mac OS* in this chapter.

How to do it...

We want to know how to run our app from the terminal and how to give it the correct size. To make this possible, let's follow these steps:

1. Locate the directory that has the files, e2.py and GOR.mov, something like:

   /home/Me/Documents/e2app/.

2. Open the file e2.py in your favorite editor.

3. After the import lines, add the following lines:

   ```
   from kivy.core.window import Window
   Window.system_size=(600,500)
   ```

4. Run the app in the terminal:

   ```
   $ python e2.py
   ```

How it works...

The third step is to state the size of our app window with the following instruction:

```
Window.system_size=(600,500)
```

We have used the usual vector definition (x, y), so the window will be 600 pixels in the horizontal and 500 in the vertical. For information, remember that the most popular resolution is *1280 × 1024* in LCD screens. Now, we didn't need to call the module size in the fourth step. This is the step where we ran the app. It opened the app window and showed the Kivy log in the Prompt.

9

Kivy for Mobile Devices

In this chapter, we will cover the following:

- ▸ Packaging for iOS
- ▸ Resizing the screen into iOS
- ▸ Leveraging mobile features in iOS
- ▸ Preparing for the App Store
- ▸ Packaging for Android
- ▸ Resizing the screen into Android
- ▸ Leveraging mobile features in Android

Introduction

This chapter describes one of the most special features of the Kivy framework, which gives more versatility to our apps. Nowadays, the mobile world is one of the biggest markets for our apps. Many users prefer to have the Internet access only through their mobile devices, and for practical purposes, the futhure of the Internet is through mobile connections.

In this chapter, we will learn how to package our apps for mobile devices. Again, we will use the same code for our app on both the platforms (iOS and Android) and take advantage of the features provided by the mobile device world. We will check the screen size and decide how to make use of the mobile devices in our apps.

Also, Kivy is one of the unique means to run Python on Android. Considering that you have read all the previous chapters, you are now familiar with the Kivy concepts. So now if you want to create mobile apps to be registered in the App Store of your preference, then go through the recipes in this chapter. They will help you achieve that.

Packaging for iOS

iOS devices are probably the most popular mobile devices. So, it is important to learn how to distribute our app on this platform. Even though we do not have to change the code for our app, we need to generate a package with Python, Kivy, and the additional libraries in order to run our app on an iOS device. In this recipe, we are going to learn how to package a simple app that does not require additional libraries.

Getting ready

First, you must enroll in the iOS developer program to test the app packaged on a real iOS device. If you are not already a part of this program, visit `https://developer.apple.com/programs/ios/` to learn how to enroll in it.

Second, we need to install `kivy-iOS` in the OS X machine that we are working on. This compilation of Kivy has the following dependencies:

- autoconf
- automake
- libtool
- pkg-config
- Cython (version 0.21.2)
- git

After getting them installed on the OS X machine, we must get the `kivy-iOS` from the terminal to the folder of our choice:

```
$ git clone git://github.com/kivy/kivy-ios
```

After this, enter the `kivy-ios` folder:

```
$ cd kivy-ios
```

Here we compile the distribution with:

```
$ ./toolchain.py build kivy
```

Now we are ready for the `kivy-iOS` distribution to be packaged with our app.

Next, we need an app to be packaged. In this recipe, we will use the similar app as the one used in the recipe *Evolving to the touchscreen* in *Chapter 2, Input, Motion, and Touch*. We will use two files. The first is the Python file named `main.py`:

```python
# main.py
import kivy
kivy.require('1.9.0') # code tested in this kivy version !

from kivy.app import App
from kivy.uix.widget import Widget

class MyW(Widget):

    def on_touch_down(self, touch):
        if 'button' in touch.profile:
            self.ids.button1.text = touch.button

        self.ids.label1.text = str(touch.profile)
class e1App(App):

    def build(self):
        return MyW()

if __name__ == '__main__':
    e1App().run()
```

The second is the KV file named `e1.kv`:

```
# e1.kv
<MyW>:
    Button:
        id: button1
        text: 'Hello'
    Label:
        id: label1
        pos: 100, 100
        text: 'My label before press the screen'
```

Finally, we need to install the latest version of Apple Xcode, which is the gate to the iOS device. At the time of writing, `kivy-iOS` cannot run in the Xcode iOS simulator, so we need a real iOS device.

How to do it...

In this recipe, we are going to create a package to be run on an iOS device. We will use two files for the app: `main.py` and `e1.kv`. To complete this recipe, we are going to work directly on the terminal. Follow these steps:

1. Go to the `kivy-ios` folder.

2. Create the package:

```
$ ./toolchain.py create MyApp ~/myapp/
```

3. Open the Xcode project:

```
$ open MyApp-ios/MyApp.xcodeproj
```

4. Run it with the play button in Xcode.

How it works...

The first step was what we covered in the *getting ready* section of this recipe. It was a one-time action, which made the packaging process simpler.

The second step basically created the package. The third term (`MyApp`) corresponds to the name of our app, and the fourth term is the location of the source of our app in the computer. One very important aspect is that you have to ensure that the entry point of your application is a file named `main.py`.

The third step opened the Xcode project with the correct configuration. We actually do not have to edit our code in Xcode because it is already packaged. We used only Xcode to load our app into the iOS device. It is important that whenever you make a change in the app's code, you must repeat the entire recipe.

In the fourth step, the package was loaded into the iOS device. After this, you may disconnect the iOS device and use the app in it.

There's more...

You can customize your package by minimizing the `zip` file in `build/python/lib/python27.zip`. This contains all the Python modules. You can edit the `zip` file and remove all the files if your app is not using them.

See also

If you are interested in knowing more about compiling the `kivy-iOS`, then you can visit `http://kivy.org/docs/guide/packaging-ios-compile.html#packaging-ios-compile`.

Resizing the screen into iOS

When you run your app in the iOS device, you will note how different it looks from on the screen of your computer. Some widgets could not fit in the screen, and the location of them may change. In this recipe, we will learn how to address this situation using a simple app.

Getting ready

In this recipe, we are going to use the same code which was used in the previous recipe. Also, it is important to read the earlier recipe to know how to run your code in a real iOS device.

How to do it...

Now we have the two files: the `main.py` file that is the Python file with the operational part of the app and the `e1.kv` file that is the KV file with the graphical aspects of the app. If we want to improve our app design, we can run it like this:

```
$ python main.py -m screen:ipad3
```

If we want to see it as on an iPhone, we use this:

```
$ python main.py -m screen:iphone5,portrait
```

How it works...

We used the module screen that permits us to simulate the screen of the most common iOS devices. If we run it without the module, the app will be like this:

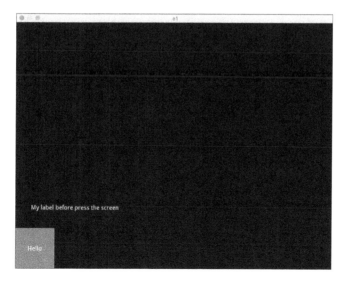

If we run it using the screen module, we will see this:

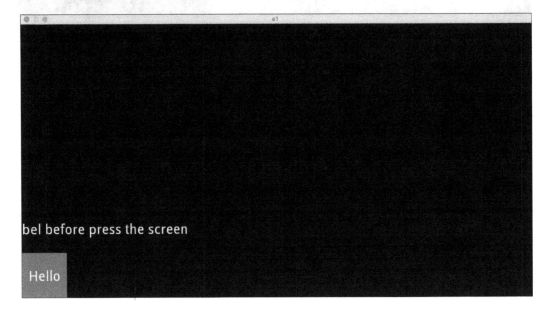

So, with this simple step, we can note some small mistakes that we could have made without running the app in the iOS device.

The default option for the screen module is to simulate the display as landscape, so this is why, we should use the portrait option to simulate a portrait display.

While developing cross-platform apps, we have to take this topic seriously because we do not want our apps to look different depending on the platform that is used. This is highly related to responsive web design, which aims to craft sites with optimal viewing and interaction experiences across a wide range of device displays.

There's more...

You can simulate these iOS displays in the following screen modules:

- iPad
- iPad 3
- iPhone 4
- iPhone 5

See also

If you want to know more about this module, visit `http://kivy.org/docs/api-kivy.modules.screen.html`, and `https://en.wikipedia.org/wiki/Responsive_web_design` for responsive web design information.

Leveraging mobile features in iOS

There are a lot of features that mobile devices have nowadays. In this recipe, we will learn how to take advantage of this in our iOS apps. Also, we will use the accelerometer in the iOS app.

Getting ready

We will create an iOS package in this recipe. Thus, you should read the recipe *Packaging for iOS* in this chapter. In this app, we will also use code similar to that used in the recipe *Working with the accelerometer* in *Chapter 2, Input, Motion, and Touch*. We will need a KV file, which we will name `e2.kv`:

```
<Acce>:
    Label:
        id: label1
        pos: 150, 300
        text: 'X: '

    Label:
        id: label2
        pos: 150, 250
        text: 'Y: '

    Label:
        id: label3
        pos: 150, 200
        text: 'Z: '

    Label:
        id: status
        pos: 150, 150
        text: ''

    Button:
        id: button1
        pos: 150, 50
        text: 'Start'
        on_press: root.pressed1()
```

We will also need the Python file, `main.py`:

```python
import kivy
kivy.require('1.9.0') # code tested in this kivy version !
from kivy.app import App
from kivy.properties import ObjectProperty
from kivy.uix.widget import Widget
from kivy.clock import Clock

from plyer import accelerometer

class Acce(Widget):
    def __init__(self):
        super(Acce, self).__init__()
        self.sensorEnabled = False

    def pressed1(self):
        try:
            if not self.sensorEnabled:
                accelerometer.enable()
                Clock.schedule_interval(self.get_acceleration, 1
                / 20.)

                self.sensorEnabled = True
                self.ids.button1.text = "Stop"
            else:
                accelerometer.disable()
                Clock.unschedule(self.get_acceleration)

                self.sensorEnabled = False
                self.ids.button1.text = "Start"
        except NotImplementedError:
            import traceback; traceback.print_exc()
            self.ids.status.text = "Accelerometer is not
            supported for your platform"

    def get_acceleration(self, dt):
        val = accelerometer.acceleration
        self.ids.label1.text = "X: " + str(val[0])
        self.ids.label2.text = "Y: " + str(val[1])
        self.ids.label3.text = "Z: " + str(val[2])

class e2App(App):
    def build(self):
        return Acce()

if __name__ == '__main__':
    e2App().run()
```

How to do it...

Here, we are going to package our app with an additional library to leverage some mobile features. We have the Python and KV files with all the graphical interface aspects. Let's follow the next steps in the terminal:

1. Go to the `kivy-ios` folder.

2. Create the package:

   ```
   $ ./toolchain.py create MyApp ~/myapp/
   ```

3. Build the `plyer` package:

   ```
   $ ./toolchain.py build plyer
   ```

4. Update the `MyApp` package with `plyer` as:

   ```
   $ ./toolchain.py update MyApp-ios
   ```

5. Open the Xcode project:

   ```
   $ open MyApp-ios/MyApp.xcodeproj
   ```

6. Run it, with the play button in Xcode.

How it works...

The third step was new in this recipe. With this, we built the `plyer` package that gives us access to the accelerometer.

The fourth step was important because it updated our package to use the `plyer` package. In the last step, the package was loaded in the iOS device. After this, you may disconnect the iOS device and use the app in it.

There's more...

The `plyer` package permits us to use the following mobile features in iOS:

- Accelerometer
- GPS
- Text to speech
- E-mail (open mail client)
- Compass
- Unique ID (IMEI or SN)
- Gyroscope
- Battery

See also

If you want to know more about `plyer`, visit `https://plyer.readthedocs.org/en/latest/`.

Preparing for the App Store

The final step of our app's distribute chain in iOS is the App Store. In this recipe, we will review some important aspects related to submitting our app to the App Store.

Getting ready

In this recipe, we need an already packaged app, so we will use the one in recipe *Packaging for iOS* in this chapter.

How to do it...

The App Store is the only mean by which we will make our app available to the users and is a little tricky process. If our app is ready for the App Store, then we must perform the following tweaks:

1. Visit the App Review site:

   `https://developer.apple.com/app-store/review/`

2. Personalize the icon for your app in Xcode.

3. Minimize the `build/python/lib/python27.zip` file.

4. Put the images in the resources folder in Xcode (not in your application folder).

5. Visit the **iTunes Connect** page at the following:

   `https://itunesconnect.apple.com/WebObjects/iTunesConnect.woa`

How it works...

In this recipe, the first step was probably the most important step. Please read the document carefully because Apple used to reject apps for some simple reasons, and this is a good point to start to figure out some of those reasons. The second important thing was to give our app its own personality, and you should do this personalization using Xcode, which is simply the process. The third step is not fundamental, but it is a courtesy to the user; the smaller the file, the faster the execution.

The fourth step was important because it solved the problem between the landscape and portrait images. The last step was the gate to put our app in the App Store.

See also

If you want to know more about the App Store and all the requirements, visit:
`https://developer.apple.com/app-store/`

Packaging for Android

Android is also a popular platform for developers. With Kivy, we can use Android as the first step for our app into the mobile world because we can test it on Android. When we know that it is working and popular, we can release our app in the iOS sector without additional programming and deliver the app to as many users as possible. In this recipe, we shall create a package for Android with a simple app.

Getting ready

We need to install Buildozer to create the package. From the shell in the selected location, let's run:

`$ git clone https://github.com/kivy/buildozer.git`

Now go to the `buildozer` folder:

`$ cd buildozer`

Finally, we set up Buildozer with:

`$ sudo python setup.py install`

We also need to install `python-for-android`. We do it from this shell:

`$ git clone git://github.com/kivy/python-for-android`

We build our distribution with:

`$ ./distribute.sh -m "kivy"`

Finally, we need an app to be packaged. In this recipe, we will use similar app as used in the recipe *Evolving to the touchscreen* in *Chapter 2, Input, Motion, and Touch*. We will use two files. The first is the Python file named `main.py`:

```
# __version__ = '1.0'
# main.py
import kivy
kivy.require('1.9.0') # Code tested in this kivy version !

from kivy.app import App
```

```
from kivy.uix.widget import Widget

class MyW(Widget):

    def on_touch_down(self, touch):
        if 'button' in touch.profile:
            self.ids.button1.text = touch.button

        self.ids.label1.text = str(touch.profile)

class e1App(App):

    def build(self):
        return MyW()

if __name__ == '__main__':
    e1App().run()
```

The second is the KV file named e1.kv:

```
# e1.kv
<MyW>:
    Button:
        id: button1
        text: 'Hello'
    Label:
        id: label1
        pos: 100, 100
        text: 'My label before press the screen'
```

How to do it...

We are going to work in the folder where the two files, main.py and e1.kv, are located. We also need to modify a file created by Buildozer. Let's follow these steps:

1. Go to your app folder.

2. Create the specification file:

   $ buildozer init

3. Open it; it looks like:

   ```
   [app]

   # (str) Title of your application
   ```

```
title = My Application

# (str) Package name
package.name = myapp

# (str) Package domain (needed for android/ios packaging)
package.domain = org.test

# (str) Source code where the main.py live
source.dir = .

# (list) Source files to include (let empty to include all
the files)
source.include_exts = py,png,jpg,kv,atlas

# (list) Source files to exclude (let empty to not exclude
anything)
#source.exclude_exts = spec

# (list) List of directory to exclude (let empty to not
exclude anything)
#source.exclude_dirs = tests, bin

# (list) List of exclusions using pattern matching
#source.exclude_patterns = license,images/*/*.jpg

# (str) Application versioning (method 1)
version.regex = __version__ = ['"](.*)['"]
version.filename = %(source.dir)s/main.py

# (str) Application versioning (method 2)
# version = 1.2.0

# (list) Application requirements
# comma seperated e.g. requirements = sqlite3,kivy
requirements = kivy

# (str) Custom source folders for requirements
# Sets custom source for any requirements with recipes
# requirements.source.kivy = ../../kivy

# (list) Garden requirements
#garden_requirements =
```

```
# (str) Presplash of the application
#presplash.filename = %(source.dir)s/data/presplash.png

# (str) Icon of the application
#icon.filename = %(source.dir)s/data/icon.png

# (str) Supported orientation (one of landscape, portrait
or all)
orientation = landscape

# (bool) Indicate if the application should be fullscreen
or not
fullscreen = 1


#
# Android specific
#

# (list) Permissions
#android.permissions = INTERNET

# (int) Android API to use
#android.api = 14

# (int) Minimum API required (8 = Android 2.2 devices)
#android.minapi = 8

# (int) Android SDK version to use
#android.sdk = 21

# (str) Android NDK version to use
#android.ndk = 9c

# (bool) Use --private data storage (True) or --dir public
storage (False)
#android.private_storage = True

# (str) Android NDK directory (if empty, it will be
automatically downloaded.)
#android.ndk_path =

# (str) Android SDK directory (if empty, it will be
automatically downloaded.)
```

```
#android.sdk_path =

# (str) python-for-android git clone directory (if empty,
it will be automatically cloned from github)
#android.p4a_dir =

# (list) python-for-android whitelist
#android.p4a_whitelist =

# (str) Android entry point, default is ok for Kivy-based
app
#android.entrypoint = org.renpy.android.PythonActivity

# (list) List of Java .jar files to add to the libs so that
pyjnius can access
# their classes. Don't add jars that you do not need, since
extra jars can slow
# down the build process. Allows wildcards matching, for
example:
# OUYA-ODK/libs/*.jar
#android.add_jars = foo.jar,bar.jar,path/to/more/*.jar

# (list) List of Java files to add to the android project
(can be java or a
# directory containing the files)
#android.add_src =

# (str) python-for-android branch to use, if not master,
useful to try
# not yet merged features.
#android.branch = master

# (str) OUYA Console category. Should be one of GAME or APP
# If you leave this blank, OUYA support will not be enabled
#android.ouya.category = GAME

# (str) Filename of OUYA Console icon. It must be a 732x412
png image.
#android.ouya.icon.filename =
%(source.dir)s/data/ouya_icon.png

# (str) XML file to include as an intent filters in
<activity> tag
#android.manifest.intent_filters =
```

```
# (list) Android additionnal libraries to copy into
libs/armeabi
#android.add_libs_armeabi = libs/android/*.so
#android.add_libs_armeabi_v7a = libs/android-v7/*.so
#android.add_libs_x86 = libs/android-x86/*.so
#android.add_libs_mips = libs/android-mips/*.so


# (bool) Indicate whether the screen should stay on
# Don't forget to add the WAKE_LOCK permission if you set
this to True
#android.wakelock = False


# (list) Android application meta-data to set (key=value
format)
#android.meta_data =


# (list) Android library project to add (will be added in
the
# project.properties automatically.)
#android.library_references =


#
# iOS specific
#


# (str) Name of the certificate to use for signing the
debug version
# Get a list of available identities:
buildozeri+slist_identities
#ios.codesign.debug = "iPhone Developer:
<lastname><firstname> (<hexstring>)"


# (str) Name of the certificate to use for signing the
release version
#ios.codesign.release = %(ios.codesign.debug)s



[buildozer]

# (int) Log level (0 = error only, 1 = info, 2 = debug
(with command output))
log_level = 1


# (int) Display warning if buildozer is run as root (0 =
False, 1 = True)
```

```
warn_on_root = 1


#       --------------------------------------------------------------
---------------
#     List as sections
#
#     You can define all the "list" as [section:key].
#     Each line will be considered as a option to the list.
#     Let's take [app] / source.exclude_patterns.
#     Instead of doing:
#
#[app]
#source.exclude_patterns =
license,data/audio/*.wav,data/images/original/*
#
#     This can be translated into:
#
#[app:source.exclude_patterns]
#license
#data/audio/*.wav
#data/images/original/*
#



#       --------------------------------------------------------------
---------------
#     Profiles
#
#     You can extend section / key with a profile
#     For example, you want to deploy a demo version of your
application without
#     HD content. You could first change the title to add
"(demo)" in the name
#     and extend the excluded directories to remove the HD
content.
#
#[app@demo]
#title = My Application (demo)
#
#[app:source.exclude_patterns@demo]
#images/hd/*
#
#     Then, invoke the command line with the "demo" profile:
#
#buildozer --profile demo android debug
```

4. Edit the line of the title:

```
title = Your Title
```

5. Edit the line of the app name:

```
package.name = MyApp1
```

6. Edit the line of files to include .pyc:

```
source.include_exts = py,pyc,png,jpg,kv,atlas
```

7. Edit the line of orientation:

```
orientation = all
```

8. Edit the lines of Android specific to uncomment the following code:

```
#
# Android specific
#

# (list) Permissions
android.permissions = INTERNET

# (int) Android API to use
android.api = 14

# (int) Minimum API required (8 = Android 2.2 devices)
android.minapi = 8

# (int) Android SDK version to use
android.sdk = 21

# (str) Android NDK version to use
android.ndk = 9c

# (bool) Use --private data storage (True) or --dir public
storage (False)
android.private_storage = True
```

Finally, edit the log level line:

```
# (int) Log level (0 = error only, 1 = info, 2 = debug
(with command output))
log_level = 2
```

9. Save the file.

10. Create the package:

```
$ buildozer android debug deploy run
```

This procedure creates a folder named `bin` inside our app directory. This bin folder contains a file, `.apk`, which is the package that we distribute for Android devices.

How it works...

In the `main.py` file, we have this unusual line:

```
# __version__ = '1.0'
```

This is now important because Android and Buildozer require us to use version control for the app and without this line we cannot create the package.

Now, in the recipe, the fourth step was where we gave the title to the app. The fifth step was where we gave a name to the app package. In the sixth step, we selected the file extensions to be packaged. The seventh step was where we permitted the orientations for the app. In the eighth step, we informed Buildozer that we were creating an Android package. Even though it seems that Buildozer can create iOS packages, which is not yet implemented, but we have to move to the eighth step.

The tenth step is where we created the Android package.

See also

If you want to know more about Buildozer, visit:
`http://buildozer.readthedocs.org/en/latest/`.

Also, you can use the Kivy Launcher if you want to run your app in Android without packaging it. Find more information on this at the following:

`https://play.google.com/store/apps/details?id=org.kivy.pygame`

Resizing the screen into Android

Android is a completely diverse forest of devices. So, it is very useful to emulate the different screens available. In this recipe, we are going to run our app to emulate different device screens.

Getting ready

We will use the same code that we used in our previous recipe. Also, it is important to read it, if you want to know how to run your code on a real Android device.

How to do it...

Now, we have two files: the `main.py` file, the Python file with the operational part of the app, and the `e1.kv` file, the KV file with the graphical aspects of the app. If we want to improve our app design, we can run it like this:

```
$ python main.py -m screen:nexus7.2
```

Otherwise, if we want to see it as on a phone, we use:

```
$ python main.py -m screen:s3,portrait
```

How it works...

We used the Kivy module screen that permits us to simulate the screen of the most common Android devices. If we run the app without the module, we will see an incorrect visualization of the app on the Android screen that hides some mistakes. Also, it helps to create better interfaces.

The default option for the screen module is to simulate the display as landscape, but we can use the portrait option to simulate a portrait display.

There's more...

You can simulate the following Android displays on the screen module:

- ▶ nexus7.2: Nexus 7 (2013 version)
- ▶ note2: Galaxy Note II
- ▶ xoom: MotoloraXoom
- ▶ one: HTC One
- ▶ nexus4: Nexus 4
- ▶ nexus7: Nexus 7 (2012 version)
- ▶ onexHTC: One X
- ▶ droid2: Motolora Droid 2
- ▶ s3: Galaxy SIII
- ▶ onesv: HTC One SV
- ▶ xperiae: Xperia E

If you want to know more about this module, visit
`http://kivy.org/docs/api-kivy.modules.screen.html`.

Leveraging mobile features in Android

There are a lot of features that mobile devices have nowadays. In this recipe, we will learn how to take advantage of those features in our app. We will use the accelerometer in an Android app.

Getting ready

We will create an Android package in this recipe. Thus, you should read the recipe *Packaging for Android* in this chapter. We also will use similar code in this app to that in recipe *Working with the accelerometer* in *Chapter 2, Input, Motion, and Touch*. We need the KV file, `e2.kv`:

```
#e2.kv
<Acce>:
    Label:
        id: label1
        pos: 150, 300
        text: 'X: '

    Label:
        id: label2
        pos: 150, 250
        text: 'Y: '

    Label:
        id: label3
        pos: 150, 200
        text: 'Z: '

    Label:
        id: status
        pos: 150, 150
        text: ''

    Button:
        id: button1
        pos: 150, 50
        text: 'Start'
        on_press: root.pressed1()
```

We also need the Python file, `main.py`:

```python
#__version__ = '0.1'
# main.py
import kivy
kivy.require('1.9.0') # code tested in this kivy version !
from kivy.app import App
from kivy.properties import ObjectProperty
from kivy.uix.widget import Widget
from kivy.clock import Clock

from plyer import accelerometer

class Acce(Widget):
    def __init__(self):
        super(Acce, self).__init__()
        self.sensorEnabled = False

    def pressed1(self):
        try:
            if not self.sensorEnabled:
                accelerometer.enable()
                Clock.schedule_interval(self.get_acceleration, 1
                / 20.)

                self.sensorEnabled = True
                self.ids.button1.text = "Stop"
            else:
                accelerometer.disable()
                Clock.unschedule(self.get_acceleration)

                self.sensorEnabled = False
                self.ids.button1.text = "Start"
        except NotImplementedError:
            import traceback; traceback.print_exc()
            self.ids.status.text = "Accelerometer is not
            supported for your platform"

    def get_acceleration(self, dt):
        val = accelerometer.acceleration
        self.ids.label1.text = "X: " + str(val[0])
        self.ids.label2.text = "Y: " + str(val[1])
        self.ids.label3.text = "Z: " + str(val[2])
```

```
class e2App(App):
    def build(self):
        return Acce()


if __name__ == '__main__':
    e2App().run()
```

How to do it...

We will work in the folder where the two files, `main.py` and `e2.kv`, are located. We will also will need to modify a file created by Buildozer. Let's follow these steps:

1. Rebuild the Python file for Android:

   ```
   $ ./distribute.sh -m "plyerkivy"
   ```

2. Go to your app folder.

3. Create the specification file:

   ```
   $ buildozerinit
   ```

4. Open the file.

5. Edit the line of the title:

   ```
   title = Your Title
   ```

6. Edit the line of the app name:

   ```
   package.name = MyApp1
   ```

7. Edit the line of files to include `.pyc` into other sources:

   ```
   source.include_exts = py,pyc,png,jpg,kv,atlas
   ```

8. Edit the line of requirements:

   ```
   requirements = kivy, plyer
   ```

9. Edit the line of orientation:

   ```
   orientation = all
   ```

10. Edit the lines of `Android specific` to uncomment the following code:

    ```
    #
    # Android specific
    #

    # (list) Permissions
    ```

```
android.permissions = INTERNET

# (int) Android API to use
android.api = 14

# (int) Minimum API required (8 = Android 2.2 devices)
android.minapi = 8

# (int) Android SDK version to use
android.sdk = 21

# (str) Android NDK version to use
android.ndk = 9c

# (bool) Use --private data storage (True) or --dir public
storage (False)
android.private_storage = True
```

11. Then edit the log level line:

```
# (int) Log level (0 = error only, 1 = info, 2 = debug
(with command output))
log_level = 2
```

12. Save the file.

13. Create the package:

```
$ buildozer android debug deploy run
```

This procedure creates a folder called `bin` inside our app directory. This bin folder contains the file `.apk`, which is the package that we distribute for Android devices.

How it works...

This recipe differs from the *Packaging for Android* recipe in the first step where we rebuilt `python-for-android` to be able to run the `plyer` package. Also in the eighth step, we added the requirement to the package for the `plyer` package additional to the Kivy file.

There's more...

The `plyer` package permits us to use these mobile features in Android:

- ▸ Accelerometer
- ▸ Camera (taking pictures)
- ▸ Vibrator
- ▸ SMS (send messages)
- ▸ GPS
- ▸ Text to speech
- ▸ E-mail (open mail client)
- ▸ Compass
- ▸ Unique ID (IMEI or SN)
- ▸ Gyroscope
- ▸ Battery
- ▸ Audio recording

See also

If you want to know more about `Plyer`, visit `https://plyer.readthedocs.org/en/latest/`.

Also, there are other projects to use Python on Android, such as QPython. If you want to know more about it, visit `http://qpython.com`.

Index

Thank you for buying
Kivy Cookbook

About Packt Publishing

Packt, pronounced 'packed', published its first book, *Mastering phpMyAdmin for Effective MySQL Management*, in April 2004, and subsequently continued to specialize in publishing highly focused books on specific technologies and solutions.

Our books and publications share the experiences of your fellow IT professionals in adapting and customizing today's systems, applications, and frameworks. Our solution-based books give you the knowledge and power to customize the software and technologies you're using to get the job done. Packt books are more specific and less general than the IT books you have seen in the past. Our unique business model allows us to bring you more focused information, giving you more of what you need to know, and less of what you don't.

Packt is a modern yet unique publishing company that focuses on producing quality, cutting-edge books for communities of developers, administrators, and newbies alike. For more information, please visit our website at www.packtpub.com.

About Packt Open Source

In 2010, Packt launched two new brands, Packt Open Source and Packt Enterprise, in order to continue its focus on specialization. This book is part of the Packt open source brand, home to books published on software built around open source licenses, and offering information to anybody from advanced developers to budding web designers. The Open Source brand also runs Packt's open source Royalty Scheme, by which Packt gives a royalty to each open source project about whose software a book is sold.

Writing for Packt

We welcome all inquiries from people who are interested in authoring. Book proposals should be sent to author@packtpub.com. If your book idea is still at an early stage and you would like to discuss it first before writing a formal book proposal, then please contact us; one of our commissioning editors will get in touch with you.

We're not just looking for published authors; if you have strong technical skills but no writing experience, our experienced editors can help you develop a writing career, or simply get some additional reward for your expertise.

Kivy: Interactive Applications in Python

ISBN: 978-1-78328-159-6   Paperback: 138 pages

Create cross-platform UI/UX aaplications and games in Python

1. Use Kivy to implement apps and games in Python that run on multiple platforms.

2. Discover how to build a User Interface (UI) through the Kivy Language.

3. Glue the UI components with the logic of the applications through events and the powerful Kivy properties.

Kivy Blueprints

ISBN: 978-1-78398-784-9   Paperback: 282 pages

Build your very own App Store-ready, multitouch games and applications with Kivy!

1. Learn how to create simple to complex functional apps quickly and easily with the Kivy framework.

2. Bend Kivy according to your needs by customizing, overriding, and bypassing the built-in functions when necessary.

3. A step-by-step guide that provides a swift and easy introduction to game development for both desktop and mobile.

Please check **www.PacktPub.com** for information on our titles

Game Development with Swift

Embrace the mobile gaming revolution and bring your iPhone game ideas to life with Swift

Stephen Haney

PACKT

Game Development with Swift

ISBN: 978-1-78355-053-1   Paperback: 224 pages

Embrace the mobile gaming revolution and bring your iPhone game ideas to life with Swift

1. Create and design games for iPhone and iPad using SpriteKit.

2. Learn all of the fundamentals of SpriteKit game development and mix and match techniques to customize your game.

3. Follow a step-by-step walk-through of a finished SpriteKit game, from clicking on "New Project" to publishing it on the App Store.

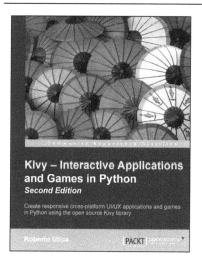

Kivy – Interactive Applications and Games in Python
Second Edition

Create responsive cross-platform UI/UX applications and games in Python using the open source Kivy library

Roberto Ulloa

PACKT open source*

Kivy: Interactive Applications in Python
Second Edition

ISBN: 978-1-78528-692-6   Paperback: 206 pages

Create responsive cross-platform UI/UX applications and games in Python using the open source Kivy library

1. Utilize the power of Kivy to develop applications that run on all the major platforms.

2. Build user interfaces (UI) and control multitouch events to improve the user experience (UX).

3. A comprehensive tutorial with simplified code and lots of tips and tricks.

Please check **www.PacktPub.com** for information on our titles